Landscapes of
PAXOS

a countryside guide
Seventh edition

Noel Rochford

SUNFLOWER BOOKS

Seventh edition
Copyright © 2023
Sunflower Books™
P O Box 36160
London SW7 3WS, UK

All rights reserved.
No part of this publication
may be reproduced, stored
in a retrieval system, or
transmitted by any form
or by any means, electronic,
mechanical, photocopying,
recording or otherwise,
without the prior written
permission of the publishers.

Sunflower Books and
'Landscapes' are
Registered Trademarks.

ISBN 978-1-85691-549-6

Olive press at Fontana/Platanos

Important note to the reader

We have tried to ensure that the descriptions and maps in this book are error-free at press date. It will be very helpful for us to receive your comments (sent to info@sunflowerbooks.co.uk, please) for the updating of future editions.

We also rely on those who use this book — especially walkers — to take along a good supply of common sense when they explore. Conditions could change fairly rapidly on Paxos, and *storm damage may make a route unsafe at any time*. If the route is not as we outline it here, and your way ahead is not secure, return to the point of departure. *Never attempt to complete a tour or walk under hazardous conditions!* Please read carefully the walking notes on pages 20-25 (including the country code) and the introductory comments at the beginning of each tour and walk (regarding road conditions, equipment, grade, distances and time, etc). Explore *safely*, while at the same time respecting the beauty of the countryside.

Cover photograph: Lakka seafront and bay from St John's church

Photographs: Noel Rochford except for pages 4-5, 12-3, 17, 18, 20-1, 32, 42-3, 45, 58 and cover: Shutterstock
Maps: Nick Hill for Sunflower Books. Base map data © OpenStreetMap contributors. Contour data made available under ODbL (opendata commons.org/licenses/odbl/1.0)
Drawings by Sharon Rochford
A CIP catalogue record for this book is available from the British Library.
Printed and bound in England: Short Run Press, Exeter

Contents

Preface 4
  Acknowledgements 5
  Recommended map and books 6

Plan of Gaios 6

Transport 7

Picnicking 8
  Picnic suggestions 8

Touring 11
  Around the island 12
    Gaios • Moggonissi Island • Gaios • Ozias • Gaios • Ag Apostoli Church • Fontana/Platanos • Loggos • Lakka • Ipapanti Church • Magazia • Fontana/Platanos • Gaios

Walking 20
  Grading, waymarking, maps, GPS 20
  Weather 22
  Where to stay 22
  Nuisances 22
  What to take 23
  Greek for walkers 23
  A country code for walkers and motorists 25

The walks (● symbols are explained on page 21)
- 1 Circuit from Gaios via Tripitos Arch and Moggonissi Island — 26
- 2 Circuit from Gaios to the Galazio Bay overlook and Avlaki Beach — 32
- 3 From Gaios to Loggos — 35
- 4 Beaches between Gaios and Loggos — 40
- 5 From Bogdanatika to Lakka via Ipapanti Church — 44
- 6 From Loggos to Lakka (via the coast) — 48
- 7 Lakka circuit via Cape Lakka, Vassiliatika and Ipapanti Church — 54
- 8 Around Antipaxos — 59

Index 64

Fold out island map *inside back cover*

Photographs and drawings of island flora

Acanthus spinosus 21; *Agave americana* 51; *Amaryllis belladonna* 36-37; *Anacamptis pyramidalis* 53; Anemone 53; *Cercis siliquastrum* 21; Cyclamen 39; *Cupressus sempervirens* 40-41; *Erica arborea* 49; *Euphorbia dendroides* 39; *Juniperus oxycedrus* 39; *Nicotiana glauca* 11; *Phlomis fruticosa* 11; *Pistacia lentiscus* 11; *Punica granatum* 11; Ranunculus 53; *Sarcopoterium spinosum* 11; Senecio 39; Sternbergia 21, 50; *Urginea maritima* 53; *Vitex agnus-castus* 39

# Preface

Paxos, measuring about 8km long by 4km at its widest point, is little more than a broken fragment of hills sitting anchored off the southern end of Corfu. The hills of Paxos are cloaked in a cool mantle of olive trees. Dark groves of cypresses pierce this silvery-green mantle. In the shade of these wooded hills lie sprinklings of rustic hamlets. But the real beauty of Paxos is the dazzling necklace of turquoise-green coves that collar the eastern coastline.

The moment you step foot on this island you can feel that your stay here is going to be both peaceful and restful. The sleepy fishing villages and the timeless countryside have cast their spell upon you.

You begin to notice just how small the island is when you keep bumping into the same people on your daily jaunts. This creates a certain friendliness amongst the tourists themselves — a friendliness that is further enhanced by the warmth of the islanders. It was this 'neighbourhood' atmosphere that outshone, for me, all the other pleasures of my time on the island.

On Paxos everything is accessible — either a few minutes

by public transport, or an hour or two on foot. Outside July and August, when there is little traffic on the island and a freshness in the air, the charm of the countryside draws you out into it — usually on foot. Everyone seems to go out for a stroll.

Here's where *Landscapes of Paxos* will come in handy. There are a number of well-known beauty spots to be seen, and this book leads you to them … and to other, more hidden corners that most visitors miss.

Being just that little bit out of the way, Paxos up until now has remained free of those obscene multi-storey apartment buildings and hotels that so badly scar the face of many tourist centres. But *do remember* that during July and August Paxos does become very crowded. Most of the visitors, fortunately, are only day-trippers from Corfu … we have the mornings and evenings to ourselves.

Happy holiday.

Acknowledgements

Thanks to my sister, Sharon, for her splendid drawings, to the many users of the book who have helped keep me on my toes and the descriptions up-to-date — and in particular to Mike Longridge and my publishers, Sunflower, for their thorough revision work.

Loggos — as perfect as a picture postcard

6　Landscapes of Paxos

Recommended maps and book

Bleasdale Walking Map of Paxos, 12th edition, revised 2015. At a scale of 1:10,000, and widely available on the island, this shows every path on Paxos! A labour of love, best used by enthusiasts: first-time visitors will have difficulty getting to grips with such detail.

Anavasi's *Paxos:* a very clear topo map at a scale of 1:17,000.

Poulin, O and Huxley, A: *Flowers of the Mediterranean.* London, Chatto & Windus.

Sunflower also publishes these guides to the Ionian Islands:

Rochford, Noel: *Landscapes of Corfu,* with 60 long and short walks, 4 car tours.

Anderson, Brian and Eileen: *Kefalonia, Walk & Eat,* with 10 walks and 2 excursions, dozens of restaurants and recipes.

Schofield, Gail: *Zakynthos,* with 22 main walks and variations, 4 car tours, and all the practical information needed in a general guide.

GAIOS KEY
1. Main square
2. Bus
3. Gaios marina
4. Post office
5. Supermarket
6. Ferry dock
7. Taxi boats to Antipaxos, Moggonissi, etc
8. Town hall
9. Police
10. Bakery
11. Boat rentals
12. Scooter rental
13. Pharmacy
14. Town cistern
15. Parking
16. Paxos Museum

3➤ Starting points for walks (1-4)

Transport

Paxos is so small that one can get around quite easily using the fairly regular **bus service** (you can flag down the bus anywhere along its route). If you are staying at one of the many secluded tourist villas, and you have children with you, then a hired **car** is advisable. Cars can be hired through your tour company or directly from the agency in Gaios. **Mopeds** and **motorbikes** are widely available for hire. And there's also the appealing option of hiring an outboard **motorboat**, to reach the many otherwise inaccessible coves and beaches that dot the shoreline. Finally you have the option of hiring a **taxi**, and the prices are generally reasonable. Check the price before setting out, however, and don't be afraid to bargain politely if you think you're being taken for a ride metaphorically. Most people, however, get about simply by strolling. And what better place for it?

BUS TIMETABLE

Gaios	Loggos	Lakka	Lakka	Loggos	Gaios
			09.00	09.10	09.35
10.30	10.50	11.00	11.10	11.20	11.40
13.30	13.50	14.00	14.15	*	14.35
17.30	17.50	18.00	18.15	18.25	18.45

* Not via Loggos. **Buses run daily except Sundays and holidays.**

FERRY AND HYDROFOIL SERVICES

The **car and passenger ferry Kerkyra** service run by Ionion Lines (no current website) between the New Port in Corfu Town and Gaios New Port on Paxos via Igoumenitsa on the mainland takes about three hours; there are four crossings a week: Igoumenitsa ticket office tel 0030 2665028085 or 0030 6948303060, Paxos ticket office 0030 2662032269 or 0030 2662032440. There is also a ferry run by S & L Ferries: Igoumenitsa ticket office tel 0030 2665021000 or 0030 2665024090, Paxos ticket office 0030 2662032269. A faster **passenger ferry**, Despina, crosses in about an hour and a half and Christa does the crossing in a little over an hour. Both are run by Kamelia Lines (kamelialines.gr), Corfu ticket office 0030 2661040372. The **Ilida hydrofoil** service operated by Joy Cruises does the crossing in an hour; Paxos ticket office tel 0030 2662032401 or email ilidaii@ymail.com.

There are also (very expensive but much more flexible) **sea taxis**: enquire at the ports on either island or call 0030 6932232072, 0030 69777629033, 0030 6944832964. They are particularly useful if you are travelling with a group.

Picnics and short walks

Who needs an excuse for picnicking on this island, when there are so many out-of-the-way coves to explore? All of them offer ideal swimming conditions and all the solitude you could possibly ask for, in addition to a sylvan backdrop which provides the much-needed shade on a hot day.

There's only one picnic spot among my suggestions where you will find tables and benches — Picnic 5 at Ag Apostoli. The rest are natural, untouched beauty spots. Some are at exhilarating viewpoints, others are in rustic countryside surroundings, but most are at beaches, since that's where you're likely to be heading.

Note that picnic numbers correspond to walk numbers: the location of the picnic spot is shown on the map by the symbol **P**. Please remember to **wear sensible shoes and take a sunhat** (the symbol ○ after the title indicates a picnic **in full sun**.

1a MOGGONISSI INLET (photo opposite) ○

🚗 by car: park near the church of Ag Marina (**8**) at the end of the Moggonissi road; then 15-20 minutes on foot; 🚌 by bus: to Gaios only; then 50-55 minutes on foot, at first along the motor road
From the parking area near the church of Ag Marina, follow the lane shown on the facing page. It is now mostly concreted and leads round to the causeway and over to the taverna and beach. But don't cross the causeway; instead, keep along the shoreline and climb the western sea-cliffs, to sit on the magnificent limestone shelves that create an amphitheatre in the face of the cliff. No shade. This would be a wonderful place for an evening picnic, watching the sun go down.

1b MOUZMOULI BAY OVERLOOK (photo on page 14)

🚗 by car: park by the church in Vellianitatika; then 30-35 minutes on foot; 🚌 by bus: alight at the taverna just above the Ozias turn-off; then 25-30 minutes on foot
*If you're travelling by bus, use the notes for Walk 1 (page 26) to reach this lookout. If you go by car, from Vellianitatika head behind the church and down past the campanile, where you meet a junction (**2**). Turn right, then refer to the second paragraph on page 28: 'Once through the houses …'. This is a very impressive viewpoint; shade nearby.*

2a GALAZIO BAY OVERLOOK (photo on page 32)

🚗 by car: park by the church in Vellianitatika; then 25-30 minutes on foot; 🚌 by bus: alight at the taverna just above the Ozias turn-off; then 20-25 minutes on foot
Travelling by bus or car, follow the notes for Walk 2 on page 32 from the 15min-point (the church in Vellianitatika).

2b AVLAKI BEACH (photo on page 32) ○

🚗 by car: park off the side of the road at Makratika; then 20-30 minutes on foot; 🚌 by bus: alight at Makratika; then 20-30 minutes on foot
Following the notes for Walk 2 from ❺ *on page 34, set out from the church (Il Conde/Pantokratoras, with its noteworthy campanile) in Makratika to descend to Avlaki Beach. Swimming in the inlet is safe, but there is no shade.*

On route to Picnic 1a, leave the car at the end of the Moggonissi road, near the 6th-century church of Ag Marina, and follow the lane round to the causeway.

10 Landscapes of Paxos

3 GEROMONACHES (photo on page 38)

🚗 by car: park at the start of the concrete lane to Klonatika (the first right when descending northeast from Bogdanatika on the New Port road); then 20-30 minutes on foot; 🚌 by bus: alight at the New Port road junction in Bogdanatika; then 20-30 minutes on foot
Six minutes (500m/yds) after turning off the New Port road fork left into an alley that descends to the hamlet of Geromonaches — cool, shady, and timeless.

4 KIPOS BEACH

🚗 by car: park above Kipos Beach; then 10-15 minutes on foot; 🚌 by bus: alight at the Koutsi turn-off, 100m/yds below the lane to the beach; then 20-30 minutes on foot
A very pleasant, secluded spot, with shade from olive trees.

5 AG APOSTOLI (photos on pages 20-21 and 45) 🛆

🚗 by car: park at the end of the lane to Ag Apostoli (well signed from Magazia); then 5 minutes on foot; 🚌 by bus: alight at the Ag Apostoli road junction in Magazia; then 20-30 minutes on foot
This is an excellent setting in the shade of cypress trees, with a picnic table and benches. From the churchyard balcony, you have a splendid view of the Erimitis Cliffs bursting up out of the sea.

6 ABOVE LOGGOS (photo on page 52)

🚗 or 🚌 to Loggos; then 25-30 minutes on foot
Follow Walk 6 (page 48) to a beautiful panorama over the limestone-trimmed coastline — barely a minute beyond the first mill. Shade of olive trees. Further intimate coves, all with plenty of shade, can be reached in 10 minutes of steep ups and downs (not recommended for young children).

7a CAPE LAKKA (photos on pages 18 and 56-57)

🚗 or 🚌 to Lakka; then 20-30 minutes on foot
Following Walk 7 (page 54), picnic anywhere beyond the second beach. From the top of the crest you have stunning views of the harbour and inland hills. Some shade. You could also visit the relatively unfrequented beach on the north side of the promontory (Missorachi; photo on pages 56-57), where it is safe to swim, and there is shade from the cliffs.

7b IPAPANTI CHURCH (photos on pages 14 and 47)

🚗 by car: Coming from Lakka, turn right after 1km on a signposted concrete lane. Just over 0.5km along turn right on a narrower lane; it ends after a couple of hundred metres (parking space for a couple of cars). Allow 5-10 minutes on foot to the church; 🚌 to Lakka; then 30-40 minutes on foot (follow notes for motorists above)
Picnic on the walls below the grand campanile. Peaceful spot; ample shade.

8 ANTIPAXOS (photo on pages 62-63)

⛴ by taxi boat; 10-20 minutes on foot
Leave the taxi boat at Vrika and follow the track towards Vigla. Take the first turn-off left (a track, one minute uphill). This track/path leads down to a lovely small cove called Messovrika (no shade). Most people continue to Voutoumi Beach — the real beauty spot — so it is likely to be crowded in high season. You can easily get to Voutoumi by taking the track inland from Vrika. Follow it round to the left at the top and then down around the headland. At the bottom turn left to Voutoumi. Bella Vista bar, above the beach, has a wonderful view from the hillside overlooking the beach, with shade nearby. But it can still be very hot.

☀ Touring

Paxos is not an ideal island for touring by car — there are no great sights or sites to see and, besides, it's only 9.5km long by 3km wide.

Cars can be rented through the tour companies or the agency in Gaios but, unless you consider a car essential for your holiday, I advise against it. You can tour on **mopeds** or **motorbikes** and, yes, people of all ages get about this way on the island. Moreover, nearly all the scenic spots on the island are within a short stroll from the **bus** route.

If and when you hire a vehicle, there are important things to remember: always check it out before taking it on the road and report any dents and scratches, etc, lest you find that you get the blame for them. Have you got the necessaries: spare tyre, jack, enough petrol, the telephone numbers of the rental firm (both for office hours and after hours)? Do the lights work? *Read* the rental conditions and the insurance coverage documents.

Important: On Paxos some of the mopeds and bikes (or outboard motorboats, for that matter) **may not be insured**. You are liable for any damage you incur, and *it is always their estimate*. Be warned, too, that some of the mopeds and motorbikes may not be in good condition, especially by the end of summer. Drive carefully, as there are a lot of novice riders on the roads, and in July and August getting around can be akin to a Shanghai rush hour. One final caution: there are only two **petrol stations** on the island, one just outside Gaios and the other at Magazia (both likely to be closed Sundays/holidays).

Pistacia lentiscus

Phlomis fruticosa
(Jerusalem sage)

Punica granatum
(Pomegranate)

Sarcopoterium spinosum
(Thorny burnet)

Nicotiana glauca
(Tobacco shrub)

Car tour: AROUND THE ISLAND

Gaios • Moggonissi Island • Gaios • Ozias • Gaios • Ag Apostoli Church • Fontana/Platanos • Loggos • Lakka • Ipapanti Church • Magazia • Fontana/Platanos • Gaios

Distance: 35km/22mi; about 2-3 hours' driving

On route: Picnics 1-7 (see pages 8-10); Walks 1-7

The roads are generally narrow and twisting: sometimes we follow very small and rather bumpy lanes. Passing on these lanes is a problem. Drive slowly at all times, watching for livestock (and pedestrians near the villages). During high summer mopeds and motorbikes (and Italian tourists who have come by ferry in their own cars) jam the roads. Drive with care! There are only two petrol stations on the island, one just outside Gaios and the other in Magazia (usually closed Sundays and holidays).

Paxos is an island more suited to walking than to driving. I don't wish to discourage would-be motorists, but rather to encourage would-be walkers. Of course, if you have only a day or two, then you will want to see as much as possible. But here again, many of the beauty spots on Paxos are only accessible on foot or by sea. Perhaps that is why the

island remains so special. Under normal conditions, 35km could be covered in half an hour or so, but this is Paxos … where you will give the sheep and goats right of way on the tangle of lanes, stop to admire the beauty spots, and let time take care of itself.

Before heading to the north of the island from Gaios, I recommend two short 'side' excursions — to Moggonissi Island and Ozias.

To reach Moggonissi, squeeze past the waterfront houses at the southern end of Gaios and follow the coast. You pass the bronze statue of Georgis Anemoyiannis, a local hero who was burnt alive by the Turks during the 1821 Greek Revolution. He was captured after his failed attempt to set fire to the Turkish fleet. Your route runs close to the seashore for most of the way. Tiny secluded coves lie ensconced in the limestone-collared coastline. Olive groves cascade down the

Gaios

*Ipapanti, the oldest church on Paxos (Walks 5 and 7; Picnic 7b). There's a photograph of the campanile on page 47.
Middle: Picnic 1b: the outlook over Mouzmouli Bay, a 20-30 minute walk from the church in Vellianitatika.
Bottom: Old windmill below Koutsi (Short walk 3-3)*

gentle inclines to the edge of the sea. Barely one kilometre out of town, you pass the rather discreet Paxos Beach Hotel (▲), sitting above a cove on a hillside, amidst olive trees.

Approaching **Moggonissi Island** (4km ✕) the olive groves subside and *maquis* takes over the countryside; the greenery intensifies. The island sits across a shallow beryl-green inlet that narrows to a hair's breadth, only just making Moggonissi an island. Through this V one can see Antipaxos rising up out of the sea in the background. Moggonissi's small sandy beach and taverna shown on pages 3-31 are very popular with those staying in Gaios, and taxi boats ply frequently between Gaios and the beach.

You *can* drive all the way to the beach and taverna on a mostly concreted lane which crosses the causeway, then heads steeply uphill. But I recommend parking near the 6th-century church of Ag Marina (photo on page 9).

Walk along the concrete lane, cross the causeway, then follow the shoreline along to the left. Walk 1 visits Moggonissi, and Picnic 1a is an especially pleasant setting for evening 'dining' in the open air.

Return to **Gaios**, then continue to Ozias: leave Gaios on the road signposted to Makratika (go left at the fork on the outskirts of town, at the left of the channelled river bed). Pass the petrol station (⛽) and climb into a small rocky valley stepped with olive groves. Barely a kilometre uphill you reach the Ozias turn-off, opposite the Paxos Club (🏨) and swimming pool. Turn left for Ozias (✕). Colourful roadside gardens enliven the countryside here. Each garden has its complement of citrus, fig and pomegranate trees — and the enormous old ribbed water jars (see title page) which were once used for water storage, but are now only a decorative feature. Walls crippled by old age and derelict buildings sit back amidst the trees. The road meanders through this arcadian countryside, always in the shade of olive trees. In autumn the hillsides are flecked with carmine-coloured cyclamen, and you'll spy pockets of bright yellow *Sternbergia;* spring brings its own floral extravaganza, with deep blue bellflowers, lily-white arums, violet hyacinths and a variety of anemones.

Ozias (10km) is a pleasant country village straddling the top of a ridge. Small cottages line the side of the road. This area was the first part of Paxos to be inhabited, and the settlement once spread as far as Vellianitatika. Turn left just past the church to descend back to **Gaios** (not signposted at time of writing).

Now, to begin the 'real' tour, once again head up the Makratika road, beyond the Paxos Club passing the turn-off to Vellianitatika (Walk 2) on your left. If you were to park by the church in Vellianitatika, you could walk to two superb viewpoints: the outlook over Mouzmouli Bay shown opposite (Picnic 1b), and the equally fine overview of Galazio Bay shown on page 32 (Picnic 2a).

Just beyond the Vellianitatika turn-off, the 18th-century roadside church of Il Conde (also called Pantokratoras; ✝) in **Makratika** catches your attention with its fine campanile. The church door was made to order — the last Venetian mayor wanted to be able to enter on horseback! To enjoy Picnic 2b at Avlaki Beach, you would set off through the archway of the campanile.

The large, drawn-out village of **Bogdanatika** (13km ▲✕⊕; Walks 2-5) follows. Two more roads from Gaios join you from the right here. (Were you to fork off right along the New Port road, you could walk to the setting for Picnic 3 — the enchanting, partly derelict hamlet of Geromonaches, shown on page 38.) As you leave Bogdanatika, you pass the turn-off left to Vlachopoulatika, a picturesque scattering of houses where you could potter around and stretch your legs, using the notes for Walk 5 on page 44.

Climbing the cypress-wooded slopes, you circle below the island's highest point — a hillock 233m/764ft high. The imposing 19th-century belfry of Ag Charalambos on the 'mountain' towers over the roadside. Rising high above the trees, it stands like a sentry post, looking out to the south of the island. You, too, look back to the south over undulating hills to Antipaxos and Lefkada beyond it.

Descending the 'mountainside', you enter **Magazia** (16km ✕☕; Walk 5). Just past the petrol station, turn left on a tarmac lane signposted 'CHURCH OF THE AYIOI APOS-TOLOI'. A kilometre down this narrow lane, at a sign for 'ERIMITIS', turn right up a concrete track squeezing between a garage and a house. **Ag Apostoli**★ (17km ✝⊓✕📷; Walk 5) is a very simple church and is kept locked, unfortunately, due to thievery in the past. But you have really come for the view of the **Erimitis Cliffs**★ — one of the 'sights' of Paxos. These glaring white limestone cliffs, shown on pages 22-23, plummet hundreds of feet into an aquamarine sea — a spell-binding sight. The bar/restaurant next to the church is a very popular place from which to see the sunset. Earlier in the day, the table and benches here allow you to picnic in comfort (Picnic 5). Before leaving, be sure to stretch your legs by strolling from the church down to the superb viewpoint (📷) over Ahai Bay and its cloistered caves, shown on page 45. Use the map or the notes on page 45 ('Detour to Pounda Point') to reach this nearby viewpoint.

Back on the Lakka road in **Magazia**, turn left and take the second right, signposted to 'LONGOS'. A flock of sooty-faced and -socked sheep may be grazing amidst the trees (photo pages 22-23). When you're out walking here, bells always alert you to their presence. **Fontana/Platanos**, half a kilometre further along, is where you turn left (again signposted to 'LONGOS'). This village boasts three *cafeneions* and as many churches. Walk 4 skirts the back of this village, and Walk 3 passes through it. Notice the olive press on the roadside, as you pass by the village (see drawing on page 2). Depending on the season, heaps of olive residue may lie across the road from the press. You can't miss the resinous aroma. Paxos has only two modern olive presses, but there are still a number of the old ones about. In your strolls over the island you'll

Car tour: Around the island 17

venture upon the remains of derelict presses. The process for making olive oil has remained unchanged. The olives are crushed with stone grinding wheels, and the pulp is then strained by pressing it through a layered sacking-like material, to rid it of lumps and foreign particles. At first the drained oil is dark and cloudy, but eventually it clears. The final product is a very high-grade olive oil.

Winding down to Loggos, you pass the turn-off right to Kipos Beach (Picnic 4). Over to your left, in Koutsi, there is a ruined windmill in a clearing amidst olive trees. Short walk 3-3 passes by this mill, shown on page 14. Notice the extraordinary shape of the olive trees on these inclines. They have massive twisted and twirling trunks, and are pitted with 'eyes'. Nearer to the sea, colonnades of cypress trees line the roadside. Soon Levrechio Beach appears through the hillside trees. This white-stone cove is very popular, since it's the closest beach to Loggos.

Rounding a corner, you overlook a tight horseshoe-shaped bay and descend into **Loggos★** (22km ♦✕; Walks 3, 4, 6; Picnic 6). To me, this village, shown on pages 4-5 and below, is the most appealing of the three fishing ports on Paxos. The pastel-coloured houses lean up against one another — as houses should in a real fishing village. And how's this for authenticity: you have to sidle past the houses and squeeze between the tables and chairs of the waterfront restaurants to drive out of the village. Where else in the world would you drive straight through a restaurant? It's even more fun when you go through by bus — the diners quickly tuck in their toes! Loggos also seems to have more cats per capita

Loggos — watch your toes if you visit a waterfront restaurant!

Lakka: from Picnic 7a you'll enjoy a similar view.

than anywhere else in the world, so drive through with your foot on the brakes.

The enclosing hills make for good exploring. There are tucked-away hamlets, derelict windmills, beaches to suit all tastes, and most important of all, peace and quiet — outside July and August, that is. Climbing out of the deep valley that curves back inland behind Loggos, you meet a junction after just under 2km. Bear right for Lakka, your next port of call. Charming old villas grace the cool, shady olive groves.

Signs of mass tourism are non-existent on Paxos; however, coming into **Lakka**★ (25km ▲▲✕; Walks 5-7), one can't help but notice a couple of ominous-looking apartment buildings. These days Lakka caters more for tourists than for fishermen. Two pincers of land embrace the shallow sandy-bottomed bay here, keeping it sheltered and calm — hence the deluge of sailboats and paddle boards. Somehow they even manage to water-ski amidst the confusion of craft. But if it's solitude you're after, you'll find it on Cape Lakka, where you can revel in superb landscapes and fine swimming spots. For children, the two beaches on the left side of the bay are ideal. Explore this headland using the notes for Picnic 7a (see photos above and on pages 56-57).

On your return towards Gaios, take the wide Magazia road that disappears into a large valley burrowing into the hills behind Lakka (it's signposted, but not till you're about 50 metres along!). A forest of olive trees fills the valley floor. A kilometre along, turn off right on a concrete lane, to visit **Ipapanti Church★** (✝) in **Grammatikeika**. Just over half a kilometre up this shady country lane, turn right on a narrower lane and then follows signs to the church. *Note:* The lane only goes a couple of hundred metres towards the hamlet and then ends; *there is only parking space for a couple of cars.* You've come this far to see the church, not because it's an architectural masterpiece, but because it is the oldest on Paxos and atypical: two brothers built the church in 1601; the Ionian baroque bell-tower was added in 1772. And one cannot ignore its fine setting — high up on a densely wooded hillside deep in the tail of the valley, quite out of touch with the rest of Paxos. This is the setting for Picnic 7b; see photos on pages 14 and 47.

Cercis siliquastrum (Judas tree)

Heading home, return to the main road and turn right. At the Loggos/Magazia junction keep right again. Ascending back over the island's backbone of hills, you look down into tree-clad valleys that wind their way seaward. You will have noticed that, on Paxos, the rural villages are made up of dispersed scatterings of houses, rather than forming a tight nucleus, as they do on Corfu, for example.

Sternbergia

Passing the Olive Press Museum, you are soon back in **Magazia** (32km). Turn left for 'PLATANOS, GAIOS'. In **Fontana/Platanos**, keep right for 'NEW PORT, GAIOS'. Keep straight ahead through the village, to take the coastal route back to Gaios. This road drops down to the coast, passing a reservoir in the valley on your right. You reach the sea at Kaki Langada Beach (Walk 4) — an ideal spot to finish up the day with a refreshing dip. Winding around the eastern flanks, you pass above a couple more delectable coves, before joining the New Port road and descending back into **Gaios** (35km).

Acanthus spinosus

Walking

Paxos is ideal for strolling, a place where you can amble along … oblivious of time and with no particular destination in mind. The countryside is gentle and friendly, the cove-indented coastline irresistible and fun to explore.

Grading, waymarking, maps, GPS

We've tried to give you a quick overview of each walk's **grade** in the Contents. *All the walks in this book are graded with the inexperienced walker in mind*. And if you can't summon up the energy for several hours of rambling, have a look at the short walks (where the grade is likely to less energy-sapping) and the picnic suggestions (*very* short, generally easy walks, especially suitable on really hot days). Experienced ramblers will no doubt find all the walks in this book quite easy.

Walking

- ● easy-moderate — ascents/descents of no more than about 100-200m/330-650ft; good surfaces underfoot; easily followed
- ● moderate-strenuous — ascents/descents may be over 200m/650ft; variable surfaces underfoot; possible route-finding problems

Either of the above grades may be followed by:
- ❗ possibility of vertigo — for those with no head for heights; you must be sure-footed and agile

Important: All walkers should check the Sunflower website for updates *before* embarking on any walk. See the 'UPDATE' tab on the Paxos page. Note also that *times* are given in the heading for each walk but, in summer particularly, a pleasant amble may — perhaps should — take twice as long. Take this into account when planning bus connections.

There is virtually *no* **waymarking** on Paxos, and no signposting for walkers (although attractions like churches *are* well signposted). You may see waymarks on some stretches of the walks, but it is ***important that you follow the notes in the book.***

The **maps** in this book are based on Openstreetmap mapping (see page 2), very heavily annotated from our notes and GPS work in the field. We hope that our map, which we have found to be *very* accurate on the ground, will be helpful. We have reproduced it at 1:28,000 to fit our format, but you could enlarge it by photocopying (some walkers even buy both the paperback *and* a pdf file of the same book from our website to print out maps at a larger size). On page 6 we recommend other maps.

Free **GPS track** downloads are available for all these walks: see the Paxos page on the Sunflower website. Bear in mind, however, that GPS readings should

Picnic 5 gives you this fabulous view over the Erimitis Cliffs

never be relied upon as your sole reference point, as conditions can change overnight. *But even if you don't use GPS, these maps are so accurate that you can easily compare them with Google Maps on your smartphone and pinpoint your exact position. And it's great fun opening our GPX files over Google Earth to preview the walks in advance!*

Weather

The kindest months for your strolls around Paxos and Antipaxos are on either side of summer: April to June and September to October. July and August, when temperatures are mostly over 30°C, are the hot and sticky months — but sea breezes do help to keep you cool. This the time for short strolls only — to the beach or a picnic spot.

Spring is announced in April with warmth in the sun and an extravaganza of wild flowers, but the rain isn't over yet. By June a rainy day is considered unlucky, and in July or August, a phenomenon. Towards the end of September there's a freshness in the air again, with an occasional passing thunderstorm. In early October it's time for a fleece and, as the month progresses, the cloudy days turn to rainy days. It's not the time for a beach holiday, but the haze-free cerulean sky and lush greenery, where autumn flowers hide, make this an exhilarating time to walk.

Where to stay

Paxos is so small that any part of the island can be reached within half an hour if you have a rented car or moped. The island is also relatively well served by bus and speedboat (to Moggonissi Island and Antipaxos). The **three main tourist centres** are the ports of Gaios (the capital), Loggos and Lakka. In these places you can find villas, hotels, apartments or rooms. Remember that during the high season accommodation is *very* hard to find, if you have not booked it in advance.

Near Fontana/Platanos, sooty-faced and -socked sheep graze under olive trees.

Nuisances

The chief problem one has to watch out for on Paxos is snakes. May and June is when the snakes come out to play ... and October, to a lesser extent. When walking in long grass, take a stick to beat the grass, and be vigilant around springs and water sources in the hot summer months.

Dogs in general are no bother; they are all bark and no bite. Threatening them with a stick or stone does the trick. **Scorpions** are nocturnal creatures, and the only time you'll encounter them is when you move logs or rocks. Do so carefully. Their sting is not dangerous, just very painful. **Bees** and **wasps** abound in summer, particularly around water. Approach all water sources and ponds, etc with care. If you are allergic to stings, make sure you have the necessary pills with you. Perhaps the biggest nuisance — but only in midsummer — is the **horse-fly**. Long trousers and long-sleeved shirts lessen the problem. Avoid **ticks** by wearing long socks. Always watch out for **sea urchins** when swimming; they are found close to the shore in many coves and beaches.

If you hear shooting, make your presence known to the **hunters**. There is still a certain amount of illegal bird-shooting taking place on the island, but nothing like the slaughter of the past.

What to take

I've listed at the heading of each walk the minimum *year-round* equipment, relying on you to modify the list according to the season. You may find this checklist helpful.

walking boots or **sturdy shoes**	bandages and band-aids
mobile/smartphone (the emergency number for Paxos is **112**, as throughout the EU)	picnic plates, cups etc
	protective sun cream
	wind cheat
knives and openers	**sunhat, sunglasses**
waterproof rain gear	**antiseptic cream**
long trousers, tight at the ankles (sun and tick protection)	insect repellent
	fleece
long-sleeved shirt (sun protection)	extra pair of (long) socks
small rucksack	spare boot laces
whistle, torch	groundsheet

The items highlighted in bold type are mandatory. Please don't ruin your holiday with a sprained ankle or sunstroke. Always carry a sunhat, long-sleeved shirt and long trousers with you, and put them on when you have had enough sun. Take your lunch in a shady spot on hot days, and carry a good supply of fruit and water.

Greek for walkers

In the majority of the tourist areas you hardly need to know any Greek, but once you are out in the countryside a few words of the language will be helpful. Anyway, it is nice to be able to communicate, if only a little, and people warm to your attempts.

Here's one way to ask directions in Greek and understand the answers you get! First memorise the few 'key' and 'secondary' questions given below. Then, *always follow up your key question with a second question demanding a yes (ne) or no (ochi) answer.* Greeks invariably raise their heads to say 'no', which looks to us like the beginning of a 'yes'! (By the way, '*ochi*'(no) might be pronounced as **o**-hee, **o**-shee or even **oi**-ee.) Following are the two most likely situations in which you may need to use some Greek. The dots (...) show where you will fill in the name of your destination. Ask someone who lives on the island to help you with the pronunciation of place names.

■ *Asking the way*

The key questions

English	Approximate Greek pronunciation
Good day, greetings	**Hair**-i-tay
Hello, hi (informal)	**Yas**-sas(plural); **Yia**-soo(singular)
Please —	**Sas** paraka**loh** —
Where is the road to...?	**Pou ee**-nay o **thro**-mo stoh...?

the footpath to...?	ee mono-**pati** stoh...?
the bus stop?	ee **sta**ssis?
Many thanks.	Eff-hah-ree-**stoh** po-li.

Secondary question leading to a yes/no answer

English	Approximate Greek pronunciation
Is it here?	**Ee**-nay **etho**?
Is it there?	**Ee**-nay eh-**kee**?
Is it straight ahead?	**Ee**-nay kat-eff-**thia**?
Is it behind?	**Ee**-nay **pee**-so?
Is it to the right?	**Ee**-nay thex-**ya**?
Is it to the left?	**Ee**-nay aris-teh-**rah**?
Is it above?	**Ee**-nay eh-**pano**?
Is it below?	**Ee**-nay **kah**-to?

- *Asking a taxi driver to take you somewhere and return for you, or asking a taxi driver to collect you*

English	Approximate Greek pronunciation
Please —	**Sas** parakа**loh** —
Would you take us to ...?	Tha **pah**-reh mas stoh...?
Come and pick us up from ... at ...	**El**-la na mas **pah**-reh-teh apo ... stees ...

(Just point out on your watch the time you wish to be collected.)

Country code for walkers and motorists

Experienced ramblers are used to following a 'country code', but tourists may unwittingly cause damage, harm animals, and even endanger their own lives. Please heed this country code.

- **Do not light fires**. Stub out cigarettes with care.
- **Do not frighten animals**. By making loud noises or trying to touch or photograph them, you may cause them to run in fear and be hurt.
- **Walk quietly** through all hamlets and villages, and take care not to provoke any dogs. A walking stick is good protection against a menacing dog, but otherwise, keep it out of sight.
- **Leave all gates as you find them**. Although you may not see any animals, the gates *do* have a purpose.
- **Protect all wild and cultivated plants**. Don't try to pick wild flowers or uproot saplings. All fruit and other crops are private property and should not be touched. *Never walk over cultivated land.*
- **Take all your litter away with you.**
- **Walkers** — *do not take risks!* Do not attempt walks beyond your capacity. **Never take a long hike on your own**, and *always* tell a responsible person exactly where you are going and what time you plan to return. Remember, if you become lost or injure yourself, it may be a long time before you are found. Carry some water, food and a cover-up.

Walk 1: CIRCUIT FROM GAIOS VIA TRIPITOS ARCH AND MOGGONISSI ISLAND

See also photos on pages 9 and 14
Distance: 11km/6.8mi; 3h50min
Grade: ● fairly easy, if you exclude the descent to the Tripitos Arch. If you do the whole walk, the grade is ●❗moderate to strenuous, with ups and downs of about 250m/820ft overall. The descent to the Tripitos Arch follows a goats' path, with the **possibility of vertigo** — *only recommended in dry weather*.
Equipment: sturdy shoes or walking boots, sunhat, suncream, long-sleeved shirt, long trousers, fleece, rainwear, bathing suit, picnic, water
Access/starting point: 🚐 to Gaios or the Vellianitatika turn-off; GPS coordinates for starting point 39° 11.802'N, 20° 11.060'E
To return: 🚐 from Gaios
Short walk: Tripitos Arch circuit: 6.6km/4mi; 2h30min; ●❗ moderate to strenuous; access/return as above. Follow the main walk to **Tripitos Arch** (❻). Once back on the main path, turn off left after a few metres/yards, to make for **Ozias** (❼), from where you can follow the road back to Gaios.
Alternative walk: Variation on the main walk circuit: 10.6km/ 6.6mi; 3h50min; ●❗ moderate to strenuous; access/return as above. Follow the main walk to the edge of the cliffs overlooking **Mouzmouli Bay** (❹). Instead of retracing steps, continue to the left from here, contouring more or less at 75m above the sea, until the path bends left and rises another 20m to the 'DOOR IN THE WALL' junction (❺), then continue the main walk.

Tripitos Arch is one of the island's natural wonders. It takes you by surprise: you peer over the sheer sea-cliffs and see not far below you an impressive archway of rock hanging off the island. It requires a bit of a scramble to reach the arch but, if you're sure-footed, don't miss this descent. Otherwise, just enjoy the peace and quiet of the shady mule tracks we follow. Then cross the short causeway to Moggonissi Island and take a dip in the beautiful inlet that lights up this picturesque corner of Paxos. Of all the walk in this book, this is the one most beloved of 'Landscapers'.

Start the walk from the MAIN SQUARE *(platia)* in **Gaios** (⓿): leave on the road signposted 'MAKRATIKA/VELLIANITA-TIKA'. When it forks almost at once keep left (at the left of the river bed channel). This country road ascends steadily into the spine of modest hills that runs down the centre of the island. Twisted old olive trees lean out over the road. Paxos seems to be one extended canopy of olive groves — they cover most of the island and have done so since the Venetian era. It's estimated that the island supports some 300,000 of them. It is said that a well-nurtured tree is able to produce up to 20 kilos of olive oil in a good year.

Crumbled stone walls terrace the rocky limestone hill-sides. Around **10min** uphill, opposite the PAXOS CLUB, you pass the OZIAS TURN-OFF. Barely a minute beyond it, reach a TAVERNA (❶) on the left, on a curve. Leave the road here and

Walk 1: Circuit via Tripitos Arch and Mogonissi   27

take the path round the back of the taverna (walking through the table area), soon passing a CHURCH on your left. Just before you reach the Ozias road on the left, keep along a path above the road, on the right, and then turn right uphill on a mule track. This wide cobbled trail climbs to Vellianitatika;

Tripitos Arch

a high stone wall lines the right-hand side of the trail, and terracing litters the slope.

At the JUNCTION BELOW THE CAMPANILE (**2**) in **Vellianitatika**, turn left. (Beyond is the church itself, which backs onto the *platia*.) Once through the houses, curve left on an earthen path. Circling a solitary house with a garden on your left, you come to a junction and turn right along a driveway. Then branch off the drive onto the first path heading off to the right. Stone walls hem you in. When a SQUARE-LIKE JUNCTION with an OLIVE PRESS (**3**) brings you to a halt, head right (at the left of the OLIVE PRESS), towards the coast. Ignore the narrow alleys leading off the path.

Suddenly you're at a VIEWPOINT (**4**) on the very edge of the cliffs rising to the south of **Mouzmouli Bay**. This gaping bite out of the coastline, shown on page 14, is the setting for Picnic 1b. **Cape Chiros** lies below. Approach the cliffs with care, especially if you are picnicking — it's a fairly precarious perch so near to the cliff-edge. A footpath leads off towards the headland, but after 10 minutes it peters out in a mass of boulders and old terraces. It is better to leave the cape to the seagulls and reserve your energy for the Tripitos Arch.

To continue the main walk*, return to the SQUARE-LIKE JUNCTION with the OLIVE PRESS (**3**), three minutes back from the picnic spot. From here head along the alley to the right, to take a concrete lane which ends metres further uphill. A garden — often flooded with colour — sits at the end of the lane. Follow the paved path that heads along the right-hand side of the garden. But before you reach the adjacent house, turn right up steps (do not continue straight ahead). Follow the main path, and you pass through a friendly cluster of houses buried amidst the olive groves high on the hillside. Tired stone walls age the face of the countryside like wrinkles.

Minutes along, you descend onto a wider track and keep right. A minute uphill you're faced with a three-way junction, where a DOOR IN THE WALL (**5**) ahead is a useful landmark. (*Note:* Two minutes up the alley on your immediate right (just past the high metal gates and where there may still be a blob of red paint on the wall) lies one of the best-preserved windmills on the island (●). Inside it are the remains of a staircase. *With care* one can clamber up these stairs for an excellent panorama over the centre of the island — worth a detour!)

Your ongoing route to Tripitos lies along the major track to the left; there is usually a small 'TRIPITOS' sign here. The

---

*Or continue to the left (Alternative walk)

A typical stone-laid mule track

broad track soon swings right towards the coast and the arch. Just after passing a green metal gate on your right, a (perhaps faded) sign again points the way to 'TRIPITOS', down a footpath on the right-hand side of the track. Follow this path downhill. In autumn pink-flowering heather brightens up the countryside on this descent. Edging around the inner slopes of a small, narrow valley, you come to the plummeting coastline. More dramatic seascapes unravel; the island topples off into the sea.

Descending further, bear right — you might have to step over a flattened bit of fence. A goats' path takes you down the steep hillside. *Go carefully; the cliff-edge is very close by on the left!* Shortly **Tripitos Arch** (**6**; **1h30min**), is in sight: a towering limestone rock joined to the island by a thin arch. At least it looks very narrow, until you are actually crossing it. The descent is more awkward than vertiginous and soon you're high above the sea, crossing the arch. (But *don't* attempt this crossing on windy days!)

Returning from Tripitos, follow the track back the way you came. After six minutes, where the track swings left, turn right along a narrow path between stone walls. *(Note: If you are doing Short walk 2, or if you wish to get back to civilisation and a bar as soon as possible, take the turn-off to the left after a few metres/yards.)* After two minutes, the path passes a roofless building on the right. Continue along the path for another two minutes, to meet a wide, stony track running between walls. Turn left along this track and, after cresting a small rise (with a house on the right), continue downhill into

The sandy beach on Moggonissi Island is very popular (and safe for young children); a taverna hides in the trees.

the olive trees. Keeping down this partly concreted track, you reach a tarmac road in six minutes. Follow this to the right to reach **Ozias** (**7**; **2h10min**), where you can have a drink at the small bar/mini-market opposite the church before deciding whether to press on to Moggonissi.

To make for Moggonissi from Ozias, descend the concrete track opposite the corner of the CHURCH (where the road bends round the building). At the bottom of the dip there is a CISTERN on the right. Beyond it rise the hills overlooking Moggonissi Island. Keep straight ahead at a crossing lane/track (leading to Yftika and Agorakatika) and continue along a minor road through attractive open countryside.

After 10 minutes or so, Moggonissi — a low mound of trees and *maquis* — comes into view, and the road descends towards the coast. A shallow turquoise-green inlet separates the island from Paxos. Reaching the shoreline, turn right along the main road coming from Gaios, soon arriving at a small beach with the remains of the early Christian basilica of **Ag Marina** (**8**) behind it. Walking along the water's edge, you look down into the limpid green sea. When the sealed road ends, follow the concrete lane leading off it (this lane leads to Picnic 1a; see the photo on page 9). You circle the base of a hillock which is thickly wooded in cypress trees. Minutes on, a causeway takes you across the inlet, which is narrow at this point.

Once over the causeway and on **Moggonissi Island** (**9**; **3h**), a rocky shoreline path to the left leads in a couple of minutes to the taverna and a beach of imported sand. To the right, both sides of the inlet offer good views of the cliff-bashing sea and Antipaxos. On the north side of the inlet, you can scale up the sea-cliffs to your right, to see the striking limestone rock formations. The precipitous and curving coastline resembles a succession of ancient Roman amphitheatres: a particularly fine spot to wind up the walk.

Return to Gaios along the coast road. Although tarmac all the way, it does not carry much traffic and provides pretty views along the shoreline. Soon after passing the PAXOS BEACH HOTEL, you can take a short-cut round the back of the PLAKES BEACH. Give yourself 50 minutes or so to reach **Gaios** (**O**; **3h50min**). Or, if your legs won't carry you any further, there is a late afternoon taxi boat from the beach at Moggonissi back to Gaios, but only when the taverna is open.

Walk 2: CIRCUIT FROM GAIOS TO THE GALAZIO BAY OVERLOOK AND AVLAKI BEACH

Distance: 8.4km/5.2mi; 2h30min

Grade: ● easy to moderate. Gentle descents and ascents of about 200m/650ft overall, sometimes on rocky paths. *Not recommended in wet weather.*

Equipment: sturdy shoes, sunhat, suncream, long-sleeved shirt, long trousers, fleece, rainwear, bathing suit, picnic, water

Access/starting point: 🚐 to Gaios or the Vellianitatika turn-off; GPS coordinates for starting point 39° 11.802'N, 20° 11.060'E.
To return: 🚐 from Gaios

Short walks (even shorter if you start at the Vellianitatika turn-off)

1 From Gaios to the Galazio Bay overlook and return: 5km/3mi; 1h30min; ● easy; ascent/descent 100m/330ft; access/return as above. Follow the main walk to the **Galazio Bay** overlook (❹) and retrace steps.

2 From Gaios to Avlaki Beach and return: 5.5km/3.4mi; 2h; ● quite easy; ascent/descent 100m/330ft; access/return as above. Use the map to reach the church of **Il Conde** in **Makratika** (❺) by road and pick up the walk there by heading through the archway of the campanile). Follow the walk from ❺ to the end at Gaios.

Picnic 2a: This wonderful outlook over Galazio Bay is reached 20-25 minutes from Vellianitatika. Unfortunately, this splendid beach is only accessible by boat. But Avlaki Beach, the inlet on the other side of the slender spit of land north of Galazio, can be reached on foot (Picnic 2b).

Walk 2: Galazio Bay overlook and Avlaki Beach 33

Here's a splendid walk to whet your appetite — an apéritif. Crossing the island (which is only 3km across at its widest point) from east to west, you sample the rural charm of Paxos. Then, once out of the cloak of olive groves, superb sea views greet you.

Start out in **Gaios** by using the notes for WALK 1, to reach the taverna just above the OZIAS TURN-OFF. Pass the taverna, and after 30m/yds turn left, to ascend a CONCRETE PATH BETWEEN WALLS (❷) to Vellianitatika. (*Note:* This is *not* the path just behind the restaurant, which is followed in Walk 1.) About two minutes uphill, pass through a junction (bearing right) and join a drive which emerges on a tarmac road beside the CHURCH in **Vellianitatika** (**15min**). Walk past the church. Derelict buildings, and houses partially obscured in plant-crammed gardens, sit back in the trees. Notice how tall these olive trees are. Some attain a height of 15m/50ft and can live for up to 1500 years!

After four minutes, where the tarmac ends, follow the concrete track swinging right between stone walls. Cypresses pierce the silvery-green mantle of the olive trees. Pass by the small church of **Ag Dimitrios** (❸), on the right, and continue along the track, ignoring a turn-off to the right. Four minutes past Ag Dimitrios you pass GALAZIO SUNSET VILLAS on the right. The track now becomes rougher and ends two minutes later, at IRON GATES. Head left on a stony path between walls, frequented by people staying at the nearby villas. Clumps of red-berried *Pistacia lentiscus* now become noticeable. The resin from this shrub is supposed to preserve the gums — and cure toothache as well. Garden plots hide behind the walls. A lean grove of cypress trees provides a brief interlude before you emerge into the *maquis* — an impenetrable blanket of low bushy (and often thorny) scrub. On Paxos this consists chiefly of spiny broom *(Calicotome villosa)*, Spanish broom *(Spartium junceum)*, *Pistacia lentiscus*, myrtle, Mediterranean buckthorn, and kermes oak.

A minute out of the trees the stupendous cliff-top view over **Galazio Bay** shown opposite awaits you (❹; **40min**; Picnic 2a). Not too close to the edge! You look across a succession of sweeping bays bound by towering cliffs. Valleys slice back off them, leaving narrow inlets in their wake. Far below you a white stony beach dips into a pale blue sea. Sadly, this enticing beach is only accessible by boat. The path quickly fades as it descends along the edge of the cliff. Go with care. Low bushy juniper shrubs dot the sea-slope and, with luck, you may spot a few swallow-tail butterflies.

When you're ready to leave this exhilarating spot, return

On our way to Avlaki Beach, we come upon some curious wells below Makratika.

to **Vellianitatika** (**2**; **1h**) and follow the road back towards Gaios. Two minutes beyond Vellianitatika, where the road bends sharply to the right, turn left into an alley descending through houses. You emerge on the main road just below your next turn-off — the charming little Venetian church of **Il Conde** (**5**; also called 'Pantokratoras') in **Makratika**. *(Short walk 2 joins here.)* Head through the archway of the impressive campanile. The last of the Venetian mayors had this specially built to enable him to enter the church on his horse.

Beyond the church ignore the wide crossing track leading to the houses on your left; keep straight on along the right-hand side of the valley. Descending amidst a mass of stone wall terracing, you come upon the curious wells shown above: one resembles a shrine, the other is conical. Beyond and below these two sits another with a large trough outside, hewn from the solid rock. Skirt to the left of this building, and follow the remains of a faint, overgrown goats' trail. Descending gently down the valley, bear left after 200m/yds, down through olive trees and then a belt of thick vegetation. You reach a wide, stony vehicle track. The bracken of the upper valley gives way to heather, kermes oak, *Pistacia lentiscus,* and *Coronilla emerus* (Scorpian senna, which has clusters of brilliant yellow flowers in spring).

Turn right and follow the track downhill; there is a short scramble at the end of the track, which drops you onto **Avlaki Beach** (**6**; **1h30min**; Picnic 2b). This secluded stony cove is one of the few accessible swimming places on the west coast of the island. Look out for spiny sea-urchins if swimming off the rocks! The bladed crest of the rocky promontory on your left (the spit of land you can see in the photo on page 32) offers you another fine view to Galazio Bay. *Limonium bellifolium, Crithmum maritimum* (rock samphire, a fleshy, pale yellow-flowering plant, sometimes collected for pickling), and *Anthyllis hermanniae* (a small spiny shrub that has bright yellow flowers in spring) sprout between the rocks.

Refreshed and homeward bound, return the same way to **Makratika**. Back at the church of **Il Conde** (**5**; **2h**), follow the main road uphill to the left. Ten minutes up, at the Gaios junction in **Bogdanatika** (**2h10min**), turn right and descend to **Gaios** (**0**; **2h30min**).

Walk 3: FROM GAIOS TO LOGGOS

See also photos on pages 12-13, 14 and 17
Distance: 7.4km/4.6mi; 2h15min
Grade: 🔴 fairly strenuous ascent of 160m/525ft at the start of the walk; otherwise easy. The beginning of the walk is *not recommended in wet weather* (when you could substitute Short walk 2 below).
Equipment: sturdy shoes, sunhat, suncream, long-sleeved shirt, long trousers, fleece, rainwear, bathing suit, picnic, water
Access/starting point: 🚐 to Gaios; GPS coordinates for starting point 39° 11.802'N, 20° 11.060'E
To return: 🚐 from Loggos

Short walks

1 Gaios to Fontana/Platanos via Geromonaches: 4.3km/2.7mi; 1h10min; 🔴 grade, access as above; return by 🚐 from Fontana/Platanos. Follow the main walk to **Fontana/Platanos**.

2 Fontana/Platanos to Loggos: 3km/1.9mi; 45min; 🔵 easy; 🚐 to Fontana/Platanos and return from Loggos. Pick up the main walk at **Fontana/Platanos** (❹) and follow the notes from the 1h10min-point to the end.

3 Circuit from Loggos via Koutsi and Marmari Beach: 4km/ 2.5mi; 1h10min; 🔴 moderate to strenuous, with a very steep initial ascent and some scrambling on the paths between the beaches; about 120m/395ft of ascent/descent overall. 🚐 to and from Loggos. Take the Lakka road out of Loggos and climb the first steep lane cutting off to the left. Keep right all the way up and, in five-six minutes, reach a tightly bunched HAMLET. Ascend the steps and pass through the houses, bearing neither right nor left. Meet a track on the far side of the hamlet and follow it. In a minute you head through a confusion of tracks at an intersection: keep to the main, middle, track. Approaching the trunk of the DERELICT WINDMILL (●) shown on page 14, you come to a fork. Take the branch to the left, which takes you first past the windmill, then through **Koutsi** and out onto the main road. Turn right and, a minute uphill, turn off left down a tarmac road signposted 'KIPOS BEACH, KIPRIANI BEACH'. Ignore two concrete lanes on the right. You pass the village *sterna* (water tank). This is WAYPOINT 5 IN WALK 4. Pick up that walk at ❺ on page 42 and follow it through a junction, over a crest, and down past Villa Chrissa. From here you have a choice of routes back to Loggos, and you can explore the pretty coastline and its many coves. (See map and notes for Walk 4.)

Climbing into the hills that look out over the harbour at Gaios, we stumble upon the partly abandoned and enchanting hamlet of Geromonaches. Sitting here amidst the sagging walls and derelict buildings, time really does stand still. Continuing on, we traipse over the island's backbone of hills. Rustic villages dot the countryside; these too echo abandonment, with their shuttered villas and forgotten gardens ... idyllic spots for day-dreaming.

Referring to the plan on page 6, **start the walk** from the MAIN SQUARE *(platia)* in **Gaios** (🔴): leave on the side-road with a brown signpost for 'CHURCH OF THE AYIOI APOSTOLOI'. The **Church of the Apostles** is easy to spot because of its leaning campanile! Pass the church and turn left. Ahead you will see the wide steps of the *sterna* (❶; the TOWN WATER TANK). At the bottom of the steps, take the path to the left and then climb a short flight of steps. Joining the town BYPASS ROAD to the New Port, turn right.

From a bend, some three minutes along, you have a tremendous view over this very photogenic fishing port (see pages 12-13) and the pine-studded island of St Nicholas. Leave the road here, just as it curves round to the left: head left up a steep concrete path. After passing two houses on your left, take a small goats' trail climbing the hillside on the left. The tall stems of autumn-flowering sea-squill fleck the terraced inclines. Ignore side paths; keep right and uphill, passing holiday villas on your right. As you climb, the bay unravels into a stunning sight, with its blends of greens and blues from the vegetation and the sea. Boats dot the inlet, which looks more like a river where it curls around St Nicholas. You spot, too, some remnants of the islet's Venetian fortress (1423), its ramparts swallowed up amidst a tangle of shrubs and trees.

The smaller island beyond St Nicholas is Panayia. It is home to a nunnery and a 17th-century church, Moni Panagias, built on the site of an earlier place of Christian worship and said to contain the finest decorations of any church on Paxos. There is a procession to the church each year on 14th August, the saint's day.

Bright pink belladonna lilies light up the shadows of the olive groves, not far outside Fontana/Platanos. On Paxos and Corfu the olives are left to fall from the trees. You'll often see netting overhead, above the mule tracks. It's tied between the trees to catch the olives as they fall. In the Mediterranean and the rest of Greece, the trees are generally beaten to make the olives fall.

Spent shotgun cartridges littering the ground testify to the wealth of birds in this area. Soon a valley slides away below you and you reach a concrete lane (**25min**). Turn left uphill, then, almost immediately, turn right on a good track through olive groves. A couple of minutes along, the track ends. Paths fork off both left and right. A SHRINE (**2**; which looks rather like a public WC) stands inside the left-hand fork. Geromonaches is still in hiding at this point. Head up to the left, and the hamlet soon discloses itself. Quite a few houses have been restored, especially as holiday rentals in recent years. But past the restorations, there are still some derelict buildings to be seen lining the crumbling walls beside the narrow mule track, and you can peer into their doorways. **Geromonaches** (**30min**; Picnic 3; see photo on the next page) is one of my favourite spots on Paxos; I hope you enjoy it as much as I do.

When the path forks just past Lithari Villas, head left uphill. The path becomes overgrown, but it runs along the line of a wall, past two derelict buildings on the right. Further up the path, swing to the right between stone walls. Turn left at the high stone wall ahead, to rejoin the concrete lane and there go right. (*Note:* If you were to turn *left* on the lane you would quickly regain your outgoing route, from where you could retrace your steps to Gaios.)

On the top of the crest, small outcrops of limestone are a dominant feature of the landscape. You have a view across the eastern flank of Paxos to the tail of Corfu, and over to Epirus. Five minutes after joining the lane, it swings right, to meet a wider road (**50min**), where you turn left. In two minutes, coming to a junction with the main LOGGOS ROAD (**3**) in **Bogdanatika**, head right. The prominent campanile of **Agios Charalambos** (**a**), thrusting up through cypress trees on the hillside ahead, serves as a landmark in the surrounding countryside.

A minute along, at a sharp uphill bend, fork right on a broad track to the left of a couple of houses. The inclines are cloaked in a thicket of greenery, with trees and bushes vying for space. Five minutes along, as the broad track begins to turn the flank of the hill, it ends abruptly at IRON GATES. Outside the gates, take the trail leading uphill to the left; there may be some RED WAYMARKS. Ignore paths descending to the right. Keep close to the wall on the left and continue uphill. When the path peters out, make for a ruined stone shed over to the right and walk to the right of it on a walled path. This will take you to a concreted lane — about 50 metres west of some ruined olive presses. (*Note:* If you are

38 Landscapes of Paxos

doing this walk in reverse, make for the ruined olive presses from the village parking area, then locate the ruined shed and the walled path just beyond it.) You are now on the way to Fontana/Platanos: turn left along the lane and follow it past holiday villas to the main road.

Turn left again when you reach the main road and walk through the village of **Fontana/Platanos** (④; **1h10min**), with its large CHURCH AND CAMPANILE on the left. *(Short walk*

Spare the time for delightful old abandoned hamlets like Geromonaches, shown here — one of my favourite spots (Picnic 3).

1 ends here and Short walk 2 begins here.) The church is set back from the road, with a large plane tree *(platanos)* in front, making an attractive square. The original, Italian, name for the village (Fontana) has been replaced by the Greek word.

Once through the village centre, go right towards 'LOGGOS' (left goes to Magazia). Keep to the road *(passing the turning where Walk 4 joins from the right)*, then pass a charming blue and white SHRINE (**5**) on the left (by a left turn signed to 'Romanatika') and, a little later, some lovely villas. About 10 minutes from Fontana/Platanos, fork left on a concrete lane signposted to **Zernatika**. Follow this gently uphill and continue past a clump of houses. By OLIVE GROVE HOUSE the concrete underfoot gives way to stone. At the next track junction, look out for a STONE COTTAGE on the left. Pass this and keep straight on. When the way ends, take steps down to a sealed road just below. Turn left here and pass through **Kangatika** (**6**) — a sprinkling of houses and, further on, a CHURCH. This area makes for some superb rambling. Continue past VILLA LAVANDA on the right.

The remains of a windmill can be seen through the trees, crowning the top of a crest below. *(Short walk 3 would take you past this windmill; see photograph page 14.)* Windmills, used to grind corn, maize and barley, were once a noticeable feature of the island's landscape; there were some 16 of them. Now, unfortunately, only the shells of these mills remain, thanks to the vandalism of the occupying forces during World War II. Walk 1 passes close to one of the best-preserved windmills on Paxos.

Dropping down into a valley through olive trees, the lane (now concrete) grows steeper — put on the brakes! It twists and winds all the way down to the LAKKA/LOGGOS ROAD in the valley floor. Turn right into **Loggos** (**7**; **2h 15min**). Time for a cool beer, and there is no better place to have it than looking out over this exquisite little bay.

Cyclamen

Euphorbia dendroides (Tree spurge)

Vitex agnus-castus (Chaste tree)

Senecio

Juniperus oxycedrus (Juniper)

Walk 4: BEACHES BETWEEN GAIOS AND LOGGOS

See also photos on pages 4-5, 12-13 and 17
Distance: 9km/5.6mi; 2h50min
Grade: 🔴 moderate to strenuous for less experienced walkers, quite easy for fit ramblers. A short but steep ascent of 120m/395ft midway; ascents/descents of 200m/650 ft overall. *Not recommended in wet weather.*
Equipment: sturdy shoes, sunhat, suncream, long-sleeved shirt, long trousers, fleece, rainwear, bathing suit, picnic, water
Access/starting point: 🚐 to Gaios or the Vellianitatika turn-off; GPS coordinates for starting point 39° 11.802'N, 20° 11.060'E
To return: 🚐 from Loggos

Short walks

1 **Gaios to Fontana/Platanos via Kaki Langada Beach:** 5km/3mi; 1h10min; 🔴 grade (initial climb) and access as above. Follow the main walk to (**4**) and **Fontana/Platanos**, then return by 🚐.

2 **Loggos to Levrechio, Marmari and Kipos:** 2.7km/1.7mi; 40min return; 🔵 easy, but along roughish paths; 🚐 to and from Loggos. Use the map to reach these beaches; the route is straightforward.

This hike takes you to the picturesque fishing village of Loggos, shown on pages 4-5 and 17. Along the walk you dip down into enticing little coves, sampling them as you go, and climb out again, weaving your way through thickets of cypress trees.

Start the walk from the MAIN SQUARE *(platia)* in **Gaios**

Walk 4: Beaches between Gaios and Loggos

(**○**): follow the HARBOURSIDE ROAD to the **New Port** (**❶**), with moored boats and yachts lining the route. Where the road swings inland towards Platanos, Magazia and Loggos (**25min**), take the wide descending road turning off right. A tangle of scrub and trees covers the sea-slopes. Epirus lies over to your right, and up ahead the bright limestone cliffs of Cape Asprokavos (the setting for Walk 29 in *Landscapes of Corfu*) glare across at you. Reaching the coast in five minutes, you pass little **Kamini Beach**, overlooked by the Anassa Apartments. Next you pass **Kloni Gouli Beach**, shingly and clean, with a small parking area behind it. Then, 15 minutes after the turning, **Kaki Langada Beach** (**❷**; **40min**) comes into view. Reach it by a wooden staircase or continue along the road and follow a track down to the beach, where there are stone tables with seats and plenty of shade. Villa Delphini sits above the northern end of this quiet beach, which most people seem to ignore.

To continue the walk, go up the steep, rocky and overgrown path at the left of VILLA DELPHINI, keeping close to the garden wall. You may need your long sleeves and trousers here. There is another wall, topped with concrete posts, on your left. After several minutes' scramble, you emerge on the villa's concrete drive, with its gated entrance beside you. Follow the drive uphill. From now on you can enjoy the superb view of the west coast and the mainland.

A steep climb now takes you up through tall dark green spires of cypress. Turn left at the T-junction five minutes uphill. Entering cool olive groves, the way eases out. Ignore the track joining from the right. About 15 minutes from Villa Delphini, on the outskirts of **Fontana/Platanos**, leave the concrete road and turn right on a FARM TRACK (**❸**; **1h**). Ahead of you on the left is Aristea Villa, a large stone house with terracotta pots sitting on the boundary wall. In five minutes tarmac comes underfoot and you pass an inland BOATYARD (**❹**) on the left. There's a small CHURCH 50m/yds off another lane to the right. Continue straight ahead along this lane, to join the main Fontana/Platanos–Loggos road after

Kipiadi Beach seen through cypress trees. This bright-white beach lights up the entire landscape.

Levrechio Beach

five minutes. Turn right; there is little traffic. *(Or turn left to end Short walk 1 with a cooling drink in one of the bars).*

Heading towards Loggos, you soon pass a blue and white SHRINE on the left (WAYPOINT 5 IN WALK 3). Then walk past Villa Anthea (also on the left). About 10 minutes along the road you pass a concrete lane on the left, signposted to 'ZERNATIKA'.* Then, about a mile from Fontana/Platanos, the road turns sharply downhill to the right, with a side-road on the left leading to KANGATIKA. *Attention!* Just 20m/yds below this bend you can take an interesting short-cut. Step over a WATER PIPE on the right and you will find a narrow, almost-hidden path. This drops down from the main road to join an old BRITISH MILITARY ROAD, with finely engineered stone retaining walls. After a couple of zigzags, rejoin the main road and follow it downhill until it swings hard left. Turn right here for 'KIPOS BEACH, KIPRIANI BEACH', ignoring two concrete lanes on the right. You pass the village *sterna* (❺; WATER TANK) behind a wall on the left, with a CHAPEL beyond it. Keep right here; then, at a CROSSROADS (❻) just past a house on the right, turn right for 'KIPOS BEACH, KIPRIANI BEACH'. Follow the concrete lane downhill, ignoring side-turnings. When the concrete ends, continue down for 100m, then turn *sharp* right on a stony track through olive and cypress trees to the coastal *maquis* behind Kipiadi. Five

---

*You could take a short, extremely pleasant detour here, following WALK 3 through **Zernatika** and **Kangatika** (waypoint ❻ in Walk 3). Ascend this lane and pick up the notes for WALK 3 on page 39. Follow this diversion to the cottage with steps leading down to the road and then turn right, back to the Loggos road.

minutes along, turn left on a narrow path at the corner of a wall. **Kipiadi Beach** (**7**; **1h50min**) is a bit disappointing (unless a storm chances to clean it up), but there are plenty of beautiful coves ahead.

Return uphill to the CROSSROADS (**6**) and turn right, now heading towards Loggos. After a short time you pass VILLA CHRISSA. About 60m/yds beyond it, directly opposite a house, descend a path on the left.* You soon pass through a cool thicket of trees. Drop down some steps, ignore turnings to the right, and continue down to the left as the path rounds the shoulder of the hill. At the bottom you reach the tiny hamlet of **Marmari**. With the entrance to MARMARI STONE HOUSE on your left, turn right along another stony path beside a garden wall. In two minutes you're at **Marmari Beach** (**8**) — secluded, quiet, and shady. From here return to Marmari Stone House and turn right along a track, to reach **Levrechio Beach** (**9**) in a minute. This cove is more popular than the others ... because Loggos is just around the corner. A few modest villas overlook this stony beach.

To make for Loggos, take the concrete lane out and turn right when you meet the road. Stone steps on the right lead down to a rocky bathing platform at the water's edge. A couple of minutes down you're in the seaside village of **Loggos** (**O**; **2h50min**), putting your feet up in a friendly bar.

---

*Or first make another detour — to Kipos Beach, another tourist-brochure cove: continue down the concrete lane and, when you reach a garden wall ahead, bear right alongside it, following a stony track to VILLA PANORAMA. The track ends here, but a path drops steeply down to **Kipos Beach** (**a**), setting for Picnic 4, less than 10 minutes from Villa Chrissa.)

Walk 5: FROM BOGDANATIKA TO LAKKA VIA IPAPANTI CHURCH

See also photos on pages 14, 18, 20-21, 47 and cover
Distance: 9.5km/6mi; 2h30min. (If walking from Gaios, add 20min to all timings.)
Grade: 🔵 fairly easy, but quite long
Equipment: sturdy shoes (or walking boots, if you're doing the detour to Erimitis Bay), sunhat, suncream, long-sleeved shirt, long trousers, fleece, rainwear, bathing suit, picnic, water
Access/starting point: 🚌 to Bogdanatika; alight at the Vlachopoulatika junction (39° 11.942'N, 20° 10.199'E)
To return: 🚌 from Lakka

Short walks
1 **From Bogdanatika to Magazia:** 5km/3mi; 1h15min; 🔵 fairly easy; access as above. Follow the main walk to **Ag Apostoli** (❹), then back to **Magazia** (❷); return from there by 🚌.
2 **From Magazia to Lakka via Ipapanti:** 5.4km/3.3mi; 1h15min; 🔵 easy; 🚌 to Magazia. Follow the main walk from the 1h15min-point at **Magazia** (❷) and return by 🚌 from Lakka.

Here's a walk *without beaches!* It's a real countryside ramble — most of it spent wandering through rustic villages deep amidst the olive groves. But a walk without sea views would be virtually impossible on this tiny island, and this walk has perhaps the most dramatic sea views you'll see on Paxos.

Get off the bus at the VLACHOPOULATIKA JUNCTION in **Bogdanatika** (⓿). You'll spot a taverna beside the road, on your left. **Set off** by taking the concrete lane leading off to the right of the taverna, with a SPORTS GROUND on the right. In a minute or two, at a lane junction, turn right; after 50m the lane turns sharp right uphill. It soon reverts to a stony surface and narrows to a path between walls. Follow the path past a stone wall with copings on the right and another walled path on the left. Passing close to some scattered dwellings, the path continues its winding course between walls and then joins a wider track on a bend. The modern central SCHOOL is off to the right. Turn left along the track and follow it for just over 300m to a tarmac road. Turn left here to explore the very pretty village of **Vlachopoulatika** (❶; **12min**), the heart of which is just a short distance ahead.

Then return past the track, go right at a Y-fork, and turn left downhill on the MAIN LAKKA ROAD. This wider road soon leads you gently uphill through pine and cypress woods and olive groves, with views down to the coast. Some 15 minutes after leaving Vlachopoulatika, at the top of the incline, another tarmac road joins from the right. In three minutes, just beyond the PETROL STATION in **Magazia** (and opposite **Ag Spiridon**; ❷), turn left on a minor road with a brown signpost for *'CHURCH OF AYIOI APOSTOLOI'*. The road becomes concrete, and in a little over 10 minutes you're in **Boitatika** (❸). At a junction of concrete lanes, turn right between houses at a sign for 'ERIMITIS'.

The little church of **Ag Apostoli** (❹; **50min**) stands on a hillock, shaded by cypress trees — a wonderful place to take advantage of the magnificent vista over the Erimitis Cliffs, where the coastline rears up out of the azure sea into sheer chalky-coloured walls. In the churchyard a shaded table and benches offer an ideal picnic spot (Picnic 5). You can spend hours here contemplating the tremendous view shown on pages 20-21 and, if you're thirsty, the Erimitis Bar/Restaurant is next to the church (if you come here for an evening meal, it may be very crowded at sunset, with people standing and blocking your view...). Those who are not in a hurry and would like to spend more time in this area, may wish to venture down to Pounda Point.

The main walk does not visit Pounda; instead, leave the church (or bar) and walk back to the junction of concrete lanes, two minutes back, then return to the main road in

Detour to Pounda Point (45min; a descent/re-ascent of 130m/425ft)
With the entrance to the Erimitis Bar/Restaurant behind you, cross their large car park and follow the stony track (part of a one-way traffic system) on the right. Turn left along another track and, in two minutes, turn right on a concrete lane leading towards the headland. The lane reverts to stone and narrows to a path outside the gates of a small villa on the right. From this point on, there are magnificent views into **Ahai Bay**. A small sandy cove nestles at the foot of a half-moon of cliffs. Further down, you can see the **Ahai Caves**, shown in the photo. As you descend, the path steepens, becomes more bouldery, and is hemmed in by *maquis*. If you decide to go all the way down to the end of **Pounda Point** (❺), *take great care* on the loose scree (the rope handrail may still be missing). If this seems too dangerous, just stop to enjoy the views, before heading back up the hillside.

The three cloistered Ahai Caves open out from the cliffs at the eponymous Bay. In recent years boat trips have marketed them as the 'Blue Caves' and the bay as the 'Blue Lagoon'. This viewpoint is similar to that from Picnic 5.

Magazia (**2**; **1h15min**). *(Short walk 1 ends in this village and Short walk 2 begins here.)* Head north towards LAKKA, passing a shop, various bar/tavernas and a right turn to a pharmacy. Leaving Magazia, turn left just past a beflagged old SCHOOL building on a minor tarmac road signposted which may be signposted to 'KASTANIDA'. You pass a concrete lane climbing up by a stone wall on the left and, strolling along, just soak up the peacefulness of this sylvan countryside — the stillness being broken only by the bray of a donkey or the phutt-phutt of a passing motor scooter.

Just over 10 minutes along, in **Mitsialatika**, turn left at a concreted Y-fork. Pass the church of **Ag Nicholas** (**5**) on the left, followed by a tiny shop on your right (so small you may not even notice it). Despite an air of abandonment hanging over these small hamlets, and some shuttered houses, there are also signs of houses being restored and walls rebuilt. Just over 400m from St Nicholas, you pass a red brick building on the right, the now-defunct Sunset Taverna. Homelier than the Erimitis Restaurant, it boasted equally wonderful views when it was still in business. Ignore another lane off left but, 150m past the Sunset Taverna, turn left at a Y-fork for a five-minute diversion (unsigned at time of writing). This stony track leads you through scrubby woodland. Suddenly you arrive at an eagle's nest VIEWPOINT (**6**) on the cliff-edge, with a dizzying drop down to the seething sea and sea caves below. *Keep clear of the edge!*

Return to the concrete lane and turn left. Follow the lane downhill, ignoring a lane off to the left. Half a minute later, the land ends at an untidy farm dwelling, but you continue along a walled path at the left-hand side of the building. This lovely, shady path swings right and then left before passing the small chapel of **Ag Isayros** (**7**) on the left. There are two derelict stone buildings opposite. A minute below the chapel, the path joins a stony track at a T-junction. Turn right. *Attention!* Only 20m/yds down the track, be careful to turn right on a steeply descending mule track with a wall on the left (a small stone cairn *may* indicate the start of this path). The path drops down into a heavily wooded valley via some steep zigzags. Just below these you join a level path crossing your route, built along a terrace. Through the trees you may catch sight of the tall campanile of Ipapanti church. Turn right on this path, which descends in broad steps to a small concrete FOOTBRIDGE over a stream bed.

Just off to the right is **Ipapanti Spring**, sometimes called 'Circe's Spring', after the woman who trapped Odysseus, turning his men into pigs. Climb the path beyond the bridge, below a high retaining wall, to reach **Ipapanti Church** (⑧). This is the only Byzantine church on Paxos and was once a bishop's seat. You arrive at the foot of the tall belfry shown below (see also Walk 7 and photo on page 14), a very peaceful spot, with ample shade. If the door to the belfry is open, climb to the top to enjoy an unrivalled view over the olive groves to Lakka and beyond, to Corfu.

With the CAMPANILE and adjoining steps on your right, continue the walk by heading along an alley between houses. In a minute, where a concrete lane zigzags down to the left, bear right along a path by a wall, reaching another concrete lane in half a minute. Turn left down this lane, passing a fine Venetian stone archway leading to an impressive stone manor house above to your right. Follow the concrete lane as it twists downhill through olive groves and, 20 minutes after leaving the church, you reach the main road to Lakka. Turn left, and in another 20 minutes you come to the placid waters of **Lakka** harbour (○; **2h30min**).

The elegant campanile of Ipapanti Church, visited in both Walk 5 and Walk 7.

Walk 6: FROM LOGGOS TO LAKKA (VIA THE COAST)

See also photos on pages 4-5, 17 and 18

Distance: 5.8km/3.6mi; 3h

Grade: 🔴 moderate to strenuous, with plenty of ups and downs (about 420m/1375ft overall). *Recommended only for fit walkers, and not recommended in wet weather.*

Equipment: sturdy shoes or walking boots, sunhat, suncream, long-sleeved shirt, long trousers, fleece, rainwear, bathing suit, picnic, water

Access/starting point: 🚌 to Loggos; GPS coordinates for starting point 39° 13.602'N, 20° 9.639'E

To return: 🚌 from Lakka

Short walks

1 **From Loggos to Glyfada Beach and return**: 2.5km/1.6mi; 1h15min; 🔴 moderate, with steep ascents and descents (80m/260ft overall); 🚌 to and from Loggos. *Not recommended for young children, and dangerous in wet conditions.* Follow the main walk to **Glyfada** (❷) and return the same way.

2 **Circuit from Lakka to Orkos Beach**: 3km/1.9mi; 1h10min; 🔵 easy; 🚌 to and from Lakka. Walk out of Lakka on the bus road. After 0.8km (half a mile), just past a steep hairpin bend to the left, take the second of two concreted lanes dipping off to the left. This lane runs close to the main road for a short time. At a fork with many villa signs (and usually a handwritten sign to Orkos Beach), turn left. After 70m/yds look for a path on your right leading down into the valley. This is the beginning of a 20-minute walk to **Orkos Beach** — a beautiful shady walk which crosses the valley floor further down and emerges by a cluster of round huts. You *could* return the same way, but for a circuit follow the main walk from ❼ back to Lakka (notes begin on page 53).

The idyllic little coves that lie scattered along the east coast make this island the gem that it is. They warrant a cove crawl, and this hike is the second half of it (the first half being Walk 4). By boat it will cost you much less energy; by foot you pay with a couple of hours and possibly a blister, but the reward certainly outshines the discomfort. Don't forget your suncream!

Begin the walk at the OLD SOAP FACTORY with the tall chimney (⭕) in **Loggos**, on the left-hand side of the port (as you face the sea). Take the broad path behind this building. A few yards uphill, beyond the factory chimney, leave the path (which only goes to the building ahead) and take a flight of steps on your left. Almost immediately turn up right on a path, which offers some splendid views across the harbour as it twists uphill. In a few minutes you come to the foot of a DERELICT WINDMILL (❶) that crowns the promontory hilltop (Picnic 6). From here you have the excellent view over Loggos shown on pages 4-5. The pastel-coloured village stands just on the waterfront; olive-clad hills cascade down around it. It's picture-postcard perfect. If you climb the old mill walls for your view, *do so with the utmost care*.

Continuing on, now swing left, following the garden wall

Walk 6: From Loggos to Lakka via the coast 49

you have been circling (on your left). Ignore the path to the right here, descending steeply to a tiny cove. Barely a minute further along, you enjoy the uninterrupted view along the coast seen in the photo on page 52, with its striking colour contrasts of dark green inclines, limestone-grey shoreline, and royal blue sea. The limestone shelf can be reached via a path off to the right here.

Further along the wall, you'll see the remains of a SECOND WINDMILL (❶) on your left. The belfry piercing the cape of

After your visit to Monodendri cove, cooled off and ready for another breath-consuming ascent, find a clear path near the far end of the beach, which climbs a bank and disappears into a sea of heather — a beautiful sight in autumn, when the hillside is a mass of pink flowers.

50 Landscapes of Paxos

olive trees, over on the right, is your immediate target. You soon pass a narrow alley forking off to the left. (You could return to Loggos this way, if you just want a very short walk.)

Keeping straight on, you pass a concrete lane coming up steeply from the right. Some 100m further on, just short of a CHURCH on the outskirts of **Dendiatika**, turn right on another concrete lane. Follow it through olive trees down to the ANTIGONE APARTMENTS, but turn left in front of the property's fence. The track turns right and then left, above their LARGE SWIMMING POOL. It continues between high stone walls, with a stunning view through olive and cypress trees to the sea below. After a short uphill section, turn downhill at a fork. Watch your step from now on, as you plunge and corkscrew downhill to **Glyfada Beach** (❷; **45min**). The swimming is superb, and on the far side of the beach are limestone slabs for sunbathing. This beach is very popular among naturists.

Sternbergia on the shady hillside above Monodendri Beach

Walk 6: From Loggos to Lakka (via the coast) 51

Unfortunately, it is no longer possible to walk around the coast from Glyfada to Monodendri Beach; the path has been fenced off, and we have to head inland for a while. Having stopped for a picnic or swim, make your way to the far side of the beach, following a path just above. At the end of the beach, pick up a rough path heading inland (there is a wall and fence on the right). Ascend the path through a wooded valley and, in five minutes, you emerge on a lane at the gated entrance to GLYFADA BEACH VILLAS on your right. Follow the lane as it winds uphill and, at the top of the hill (six minutes up), turn right at a T-junction on a tarmac road. You shortly pass the small church of **Ag Dimitrios** (❸) on the left. A minute later (120m further on), where the road bears left, turn right on a walled footpath, which soon steepens as it climbs through woodland. Two minutes along this path, with some rocky steps ahead, turn right on a pretty, level path which continues along a terrace. This path may be slightly overgrown, but in another three minutes you will take the next left turn — just before a block of apartments. Keep this building and its wall on your right, to meet a concrete lane. Turn right, and meet the MAIN ROAD TO LAKKA in another two minutes.

Agave americana (Century plant)

Turn right on the main road and, two minutes later, at the chapel of **Ag Spiridon** (❹), turn right again, on a road signposted 'MANADENDRI' [sic]. **Monodendri Beach** (❺; **1h30min**) is a fine long bay with two bars where you can quench your thirst. Have a swim and take a rest, to prepare for the next part of the walk — a steep climb up to the scattered little hamlets between Loggos and Lakka.

This climb begins near the far end of the beach. Turn up the bed of a watercourse and in 20m/yds, pick up a steep path on the right climbing via BEN'S BEACH BAR, a taverna with several walled terraces. The path leaves from their upper terrace: WHITE-PAINTED ROCKS edge the path, which is very well waymarked. This path (shown on page 49) is beautiful sight in autumn, when the hillside is a mass of pink flowers.

Splashes of paint guide you along through the flowering shrubs and cypresses. Ignoring a crossing track, enter olive groves and walk through them to a concrete lane. Follow this lane ahead (left) until you reach a junction, where you turn right, steeply downhill, on another concrete lane (where there may be a handwritten sign to Lakkos Beach). The lane

52   Landscapes of Paxos

descends ever more steeply until, at the entrance to VILLA ANASSA, you drop down a flight of concrete steps on the left and descend a short, rocky path to the beach. **Lakkos Beach** (**6**; **2h**), a pebbly cove set in the shadows of a darkly wooded hillside, is usually deserted. There is supposed to be a path back uphill from the north end of the beach, but unless you are equipped for mountaineering on loose scree, it is more prudent to return up the concrete lane.

When you reach the the top of the hill again (by the handwritten 'Lakkos Beach' sign), continue straight ahead along the lane. Do *not* turn left at a junction five minutes later. The concrete changes to tarmac, and you reach a road junction in another five minutes (with a single-storey house on the right). Turn right along another narrow tarmac road and, 70m/yds further on, turn right on a footpath (usually with a handwritten sign to ORKOS BEACH).

Picnic 6: Climb the promontory above Loggos for this superb view of the limestone shelves edging the coastline.

Some other flowers you might see on Paxos (from top to bottom): Anacamptis pyramidalis *(pyramidal orchid);* Ranunculus; *anemone;* Urginea maritima *(sea squill)*

This is one of the most delightful paths on the island and runs downhill through a 'glen', with a stream bed on your right. When alight with spring or autumn flowers, it looks like an illustration for a book of fairytales. Crossing the stream bed halfway down, 15 minutes after leaving the road, you pass to the right of the JUVENTUS ENCLOSURE WITH ITS RONDAVEL HUTS, and reach **Orkos Beach** (**❼**; **2h30min**), perhaps one of the loveliest on Paxos.

When you are ready to leave, go along the beach and turn left after passing the ROUND STONE BUILDING, then swing right after a few metres. Two branches on the right lead to private villas — keep to the main path, which runs below a wall, through a pine wood. *Attention!* Arriving at a Y-fork, bear right, uphill, onto a higher path at the corner of the wall; do *not* go straight ahead on the lower, level path which has a low wall on its left. Now climb more steeply, with a wall and barbed wire close by on the right. At the top of the wall, bear right, to follow the wall along a narrow and perhaps overgrown, level path. In two minutes you reach a concrete lane and turn left uphill.*

The concrete lane takes you up to a tarmac road after 50m/yds. Here turn right on another concrete lane signed to some villas. In about 70m turn left at a villa with a fake windmill), then follow the unsurfaced, walled track round a right-angled bend and join the top end of another concrete lane. Turn left here. The lane descends ever-more steeply through olive groves. Five minutes after joining this lane (after rounding a couple of very steep zigzag bends), you reach the waterfront at **Lakka** (**◯**; **3h**).

---

*But if you want to visit another beach, turn right downhill: after 100m/yds take a narrow, signed path on the left. This descends through woodland to the rocky cove of **Arkoudaki** (●). The narrow path continues round the coast, becoming easier to follow as it turns the headland, passing close to a light beacon, before reaching Lakka.

Walk 7: LAKKA CIRCUIT VIA CAPE LAKKA, VASSILIATIKA AND IPAPANTI CHURCH

See also photos on pages 14, 18 and 47
Distance: 8km/5mi; 3h20min
Grade: ●❗ moderate to strenuous for less experienced walkers, with some (short) rough stretches en route and one vertiginous section (which can be avoided). Overall ascents/descents of 200m/650ft
Equipment: sturdy shoes or walking boots, sunhat, suncream, long-sleeved shirt, long trousers, fleece, rainwear, bathing suit, picnic, water
Access/starting point: 🚌 to Lakka; GPS coordinates for starting point 39° 14.102'N, 20° 8.099'E
To return: 🚌 from Lakka

Short walks

1 Circuit from Lakka to Plani Beach: 4km/2.5mi; 1h30min; ● easy, but involves some scrambling through hillside scrub and a few short ascents/descents; access/return as above. Follow the main walk up to the CONCRETE LANE swinging round in front of you (**5**). Go left here and follow the lane back down to Lakka.

2 Reservoir circuit from Lakka: 6.1km/3.8mi; 1h40min; ● fairly easy, with ascents/descents of about 120m/395ft; access/return as above. Follow the main walk to the roadside shrine of **Ag Fotini** (**6**; 1h25min). One minute after passing this shrine, on an uphill section of concrete, turn left on a stepped path *just beside* a cottage. This path, between walls, takes you down into a delightfully cool and shady valley. Two minutes down the path you reach a track with the restored church of **Ag Ioannis** (**ⓑ**) on the left. Follow the track around to the back of the church and continue downhill; a sign points to 'RESERVOIR–LAKKA'. After five minutes you arrive at a bowl-shaped RESERVOIR, usually nearly empty. Follow the lane round the reservoir, on either side, to reach another track. Take this down to the Lakka road and head left, back to Lakka.

Explore Cape Lakka and discover varied beaches and seascapes. Then move on to the plunging escarpment of the west coast, an inaccessible wall of cliffs that will leave you in awe. Inland, the countryside is a timeless masterpiece. Enchanting old lanes lead you through the Paxos of centuries ago … and the Paxos of today — there is little difference between the two.

Start the walk in **Lakka**: take the steps up between the last two restaurants at the western end of the PORT (**O**). You pass below a CHURCH and then continue around the coastline to two beaches, both of which are wonderful for children.

Straight off the end of the second beach, head up into thick scrub, following a well-used path that climbs the face of the hill. (At press date this path was eroded, but users had made scrambling paths around the worst sections.) In three minutes you reach the headland track with an apartment building on your right. Turn right along the track. From the TOP OF THE RIDGE (**1**) here on **Cape Lakka** you have a magnificent panorama over the beautiful crystal-clear waters of the harbour. You might like to stop here for Picnic 7a, in the

Walk 7: Circuit via Cape Lakka and Ipapanti Church 55

setting shown on page 18. Looking across the northern side of the enclosing arm, you see Corfu, from the white cliffs of the south to the hilly west coast. A few minutes along the crest, the track ends at a **'NO SHOOTING' SIGN**. Two paths lead off from here. First take the one straight ahead; it descends through woodland to an isthmus just south of Cape Lakka, with two small beaches, one either side of the headland. Return to the end of the track and take the other path, now

Close on 30 minutes from Lakka, we slide down onto isolated Plani Beach, where curious rock 'tables' jut out into the sea.

on your right. Follow it down through *maquis* into a shallow valley. The path swings right alongside a stream bed and leads you to the rocky cove shown below, **Missorachi Beach** (❷; **30min**). It's backed by impressive cliffs, and the water is an inviting turquoise-green — but note that the sea can be quite rough on this side of the point.

Returning to the ridge track, head uphill towards the lighthouse. At the crest of the hill, a pine wood offers welcome shade. At the top, turn right at a track junction, to visit the LIGHTHOUSE (❸; **45min**). Below the lighthouse, to the left, is an unusual beach known as 'Plani'. To get there, head back from the lighthouse, passing your outward track on the left. After 150m, turn sharp right down another track. This motor track has obliterated the original footpath down to the coast, but it is an easy zigzag descent and, in less than 10 minutes you will reach isolated **Plani Beach** (❹; **1h**) and an emerald-green bay. Around the corner to the left, curious limestone 'tables' jut out into the sea. Cliffs tower in the background. If you decide to walk around on these rock 'tables', go *carefully;* they are slippery and crumbly. You can continue around the shelf for another three minutes or so, for the beautiful view of the sea caves and cove shown on page 55.

Return towards the lighthouse, but 70m short of the intersection where you turned off for the lighthouse (150m short of the lighthouse itself), keep straight ahead — until you reach a CONCRETE LANE (❺) swinging round in front of you, three minutes up. Follow this lane up to the right. *(But those of you doing Short walk 1 descend to the left here.)* Wandering amidst these peaceful sylvan hills you head through **Dalietatika** — a shy sprinkling of cottages set back in the trees. The houses become more dispersed and the countryside 'friendlier'.

The old track from Dalietatika to Vassiliatika is now a concreted lane, but is still one of the most enjoyable easy walks on Paxos. The pretty valley leading down to Lakka is visible most of the way. The lane soon takes you between two country churches, **Ag Vasilios** and

Missorachi Beach, one of the settings for Picnic 7a

Walk 7: Circuit via Cape Lakka and Ipapanti Church 57

Ag Dimitrios. Continue gently uphill, passing a tiny roadside SHRINE on the left dedicated to **Ag Fotini** (**6**; **1h25min**). *(Short walk 2 turns off left a minute/100m past this shrine.)* Continue ahead past a junction 200m further on.

The lane steepens as it enters the hamlet of **Vassiliatika** and becomes mossy under the trees. As the lane swings to the right uphill you see facing you a fine VENETIAN MANOR (**7**) linked with houses on the left. It is being restored at press date, with part of the building available for holiday rental. Unfortunately, this means that the path to a coastal viewpoint, once accessible via its archway, is no longer open to the public. So from here follow the shady *path* between walls, gently climbing the hill between the drives to two extensive villa properties (also holiday rentals). When you join a track, continue ahead until it swings off to the left, then take the path straight ahead.

Be aware that you are now near the edge of a high precipice: if you find the path too vertiginous, stay on the track. Only a metre over to your right, you're looking straight down into a keyhole-shaped chasm that slices inland from the sea. What a sight! An exhilarating, but rather frightening, lookout point! Don't venture too near the edge. The path, littered with shotgun cartridges, continues uphill, never far from the

edge of the gaping inlet on the right. A RUINED WINDMILL (**a**) peers above the juniper bushes on the hilltop ahead.

Having circled the inlet, the path runs alongside a wall on the left and joins a concrete track. Turn left downhill, in one minute reaching a THREE-WAY JUNCTION. Go down the middle branch and, in three minutes, look out for a walled path joining from the right. This is where we join Walk 5 for the rest of the walk. (Before continuing, you might like to spend a few minutes exploring this shaded path with the small chapel of Ag Isayros on the right; the chapel is WAYPOINT 7 OF WALK 5.)

Attention is needed here! Just 20m/yds along the track beyond the path junction, turn right on a steeply descending mule path with a wall on the left (it may be marked with a small stone cairn). The path drops down into a heavily wooded valley via some steep zigzags. Just below these you join a level path crossing your route, built along a terrace. Through the trees you may catch sight of a tall campanile. Turn right on this path to reach **Ipapanti Church** (**8**; **2h35min**).

The bright ochre façade of this Byzantine church (shown on page 14) cheers up this dark corner of the valley. Ipapanti (Picnic 7b) is the oldest church on the island and unique for its two circular rooftop domes. Unfortunately it is kept locked. One of the few springs on the island (**Ipapanti Spring**) is found in the little gully you crossed, behind the church. It's a lush spot. The path is flooded with cyclamen in autumn. Not a sound can be heard in Grammatikeika, the village above. The picnic spot is not only a beautiful setting, but it has also been suggested by Tim Severin in *The Ulysses Voyage* (Hutchinson, 1987) that the Ipapanti spring and glade was the scene of Ulysses' encounter with Circe, the sylvan goddess of the golden hair. Circe turned his sailors into swine, but it all turned out well in the end and Ulysses was beguiled into a year's stay. It really does sound just like Paxos…)

Now, using the notes for Walk 5 on page 47, second paragraph, return to **Lakka** (**O**; **3h20min**).

Walk 8: AROUND ANTIPAXOS

Distance: 9.2km/5.7mi; 3h

Grade: ● moderate, with a steady 15-minute ascent at the outset; overall ascent/descent about 250m/820ft. *Not recommended in wet weather*, when the tracks get very muddy.

Equipment: sturdy shoes, sunhat, suncream, long-sleeved shirt, long trousers, fleece, rainwear, bathing suit, picnic, water

Access/starting point: ⛴ During the season taxi boats leave from Gaios for Vrika and Voutoumi between 10.00 and 12.00. There is also the odd boat from Lakka and Loggos. GPS coordinates for starting point 39° 9.682'N, 20° 13.433'E

To return: ⛴ The last boats leave the beaches at 17.00. Always verify the last boat back; departure times may change!

Short walks

1 Circuit via Vigla and Voutoumi Beach: 3.2km/2mi; 1h; ● easy-moderate, access/return as above. This walk shows you a good cross-section of the island with the minimum of effort (ups and downs of about 100m/330ft). Follow the main walk to the lane descending to **Agrapidia** (30min). Here pick up the notes just after the 2h10min-point (70m before you would reach ❼) and follow the walk to the end.

2 Circuit via Vigla, Agrapidia and Voutoumi Beach: 5.4km/ 3.4mi; 1h50min; ● easy-moderate, access/return as above. Do the main walk, but omit the lighthouse by keeping right at ❸. Overall ascents/descents of about 120m/395ft.

Note: There are two tavernas on Vrika Beach and two more above Voutoumi.

Most holiday-makers on Paxos make a day trip to Antipaxos — word quickly gets around about the island's sandy beaches. Few people, however, venture beyond these beaches, and most tourists remain unaware that this speck in the sea (only 3 sq km!) has more to offer than sand and sea. Less than 15 minutes uphill from Vrika (where the taxi boats land) the salubrious tangle of vineyards and garden plots shown overleaf awaits you. Cobbled alleys criss-cross the island's hump like a great maze, connecting the farm dwellings that dot the landscape. Do the island justice — go out for a stroll.

Leave the boat at the small cove of **Vrika** (⭕) and **start the walk**. At the far end of the beach, head up the rough track that climbs towards Vigla. A minute up, you pass a track off to the left, which leads to another cove (Messovrika, from where you will return if you follow the main walk). The slopes are thickly woven in the ubiquitous *maquis*. We have a fine view over Paxos — to Corfu and mainland Greece.

After passing below a vineyard, the track turns back towards the coast and you meet the MAIN TRACK FROM VOUTOUMI. Turn sharp right and continue uphill. *(But keep ahead along the main track if you're in a hurry to reach Voutoumi Beach — one of the settings for Picnic 8.)* A surprise awaits you as you mount the island's 'hump' — quite a substantial settlement of vineyards and gardens covers the crest. At the top of the track, pass between two houses and, just beyond them, turn left at a track junction; *don't* keep straight on. Old stone walls line the track and enclose the gardens.

You pass by the shuttered stone houses of **Vigla** (❶), with their trellised courtyards. When it's grape-picking time, the island becomes a hive of activity, and the musky odour of crushed grapes permeates the air. Face-lifted cottages (and even some new houses) suggest that the 20the century has finally arrived here on Antipaxos as well. If you're not pressed for time, do some exploring, wander up some of the many side-alleys off the main route. Looking over the vineyards below you, the turquoise blue waters off Voutoumi Beach steal your attention with their alluring brightness. This beach, one of the finest in Greece, is the beauty spot of Antipaxos. The hills of Epirus rise in the background.

Nearly 10 minutes from the junction (**30min**), you join a CONCRETE LANE TO THE LITTLE PORT OF AGRAPIDIA and pass a fork off to the right (your return route from the lighthouse). Descending this lane, you look straight across onto the impressive northwest coast of Greece. Some 30m down the lane, a track branches off to the left — your ongoing route to Voutoumi, when you return from the lighthouse. *(Short walk 1 turns left here.)*

Soon you're down in the sheltered little port of **Agrapidia** (❷; **45min**), with boats moored to a jetty and others drawn up on the beach. Now follow the concrete lane straight ahead: a steep climb which returns you to gardens and vineyards. Notice the absence of olive trees on this island. After a hot 10-minute climb, you pass a house on your right set behind an ugly concrete wall topped with broken glass and rusty barbed wire. Turn left onto another TRACK BETWEEN WALLS (❸), opposite the gateway to this house. *(But for Short walk 2, continue straight ahead, following the concrete lane as it twists between garden walls and, when it joins a track, turn right.)*

Just over a minute along, where the track swings left, turn right on a narrow, stony path squeezed between walls. Follow the path down into a shallow valley and then uphill past a walled-in garden and a COTTAGE WITH BLUE SHUTTERS on the left (❹; **1h**). At the top of the incline, turn left along the track which will take you to the lighthouse.

As you follow the track south, the countryside becomes less cultivated, less walled-in, and more open, with *maquis,* gorse, myrtle and other aromatic plants lining the route. Soon after passing some isolated small cottages set in

Walk 8: Around Antipaxos 61

vineyards, the landscape resembles a heath, and you see the limestone islets of Dasskalia off to the right. More of the Ionian islands lie in the distance. Passing through a grove of pine and cypress trees, you reach the LIGHTHOUSE (**5**; **1h25min**). Circle it to the right and from the front gate, take a pathway leading down through a shady 'avenue' of pines.

The path curves left and comes to a small CONCRETE JETTY (**6**). A little cove beckons nearby on the left, but to get there

Looking out over vineyards, the turquoise blue waters off Voutoumi Beach steal your attention with their alluring brightness.

62 Landscapes of Paxos

you would have a difficult scramble over large rocks and you would need to paddle part of the way. Alternatively, you can swim off the jetty in deep clear water, but mind the sea urchins. From this jetty you can just make out Theotakos Monastery in the distance, on Panayia Island outside the northern entrance to Gaios harbour. The soft bed of needles and deep shade of the pines below the lighthouse make for a delightful picnic spot.

When you've had your fill of sun and solitude, return to the INTERSECTION where you turned off for the lighthouse (❹; next to the cottage with blue shutters, about 25 minutes back) but, this time, head straight on into the profusion of walls and gardens. Keep ahead when you join the concrete lane coming up from the right (from ❸). The track soon narrows, and you pass another track descending to Agrapidia. Follow a concrete path ahead, between walls, passing Villa Oneiro on the right. In a labyrinth of alleys, remain on the main route (which runs along the ISLAND RIDGE). After the concrete ends, you pass a path branching off left, followed by another to the right. Ignore the next alley turning off to the left and continue along to the right, reaching the little church of **Ag Emilianos** (❼; **2h10min**) on the left. A minute later, turn right downhill on the concrete lane that you followed earlier in the walk.

Now you visit those irresistible sandy beaches. Some 30m down the lane, fork left (by a small SHRINE). Come to another fork two minutes down and go right, along the top of the crest. Keeping left at the next fork and following the 'TAVERNA' signs, descend to BAR BELLA VISTA (ⓐ) three minutes along (you won't be able to see it until you're almost there). This magnificently perched bar is unrivalled on the two islands for its vista. The limpid pale blue bay and the chalk-coloured

Voutoumi Bay, one of the settings for Walk 8 and Picnic 8, is considered by many to be the most beautiful beach in all of Greece.

cliffs fringed with dark green vegetation create a memorable picture. A steep concrete stairway takes you from the bar down to **Voutoumi Bay** (❽). (But note that this is a private path and, if the taverna is shut, the path will be gated. In that case, you can either descend by the fencing at the left of the gate to the concrete stairs *or* return to the track junction, turn sharp right, and follow the track curving downhill to the bay.)

To return to Vrika, cross to the far side of the bay. Here you can climb the track shown on the map … or, for a shorter, more challenging route, go a few metres beyond the track and you will see a clear goats' trail up the headland. After a few minutes' scramble, you reach the headland track above. Turn right and, just as you see Vrika ahead, you may spot a little path tunnelling down through pines and *maquis* to **Messovrika Beach** (❾; another setting for Picnic 8). This path is narrow, steep, and very overgrown — you will need your long-sleeved shirt and long trousers, but expect to get snagged and scratched! Alternatively, if you wish to avoid the difficult descent to Messovrika, just continue along the track. On the far side of the beach, turn up the inland track and then turn right on the track back to **Vrika** (⭕; **3h**).

Don't forget that the last taxi boat leaves at 17.00!

Index

Geographical names only are included in this index; for other entries, see Contents, page 3. Page numbers in **bold type** indicate photographs. All places below may be found on the pull-out map.

Ahai (bay and caves) 16, **45**
Ag Apostoli (church) 8, 10, 16, 44, 45
Ag Emilianos (church, Antipaxos) 62
Ag Marina (church) 8, **9**, 14
Agorakatika 30
Agrapidia (port, Antipaxos) 59, 60, 62
Avlaki (beach) 9, 15, **32**, **34**
Antipaxos 10, 22, 31, 59, 60, **61**, **62-3**
'Blue Caves' *see* Ahai
Bogdanatika 10, 15, 34, 37, 44
Chiros, Cape 28
Corfu 36
  ferry connections 7
  Landscapes of Corfu 6, 41
Dalietatika 56
Dasskalia (islets off Antipaxos) 61
Erimitis (cliffs) 10, 16, **20-1**, 44, 45
Fontana/Platanos **2**, 12, 16, 19, **22-3**, 35, **36**, 40, 41
Gaios 7, 8, 11, **12-3**, 14, 15, 19, 22, 23, 26, 31, 32, 33, 34, 35, 40
  bus timetable 7
  town plan 6
Galazio (bay) 8, 15, **32**, 33
Geromonaches 10, 16, 35, 37, **38**
Glyfada (beach) 50, 51
Grammatikeika 19, 58
Il Conde (church, also called 'Pantokratoras', in Makratika) 15, 32, 34
Ipapanti (church) 10, **14**, 19, 20, 44, 46, **47**, 54, 58
Kaki Langada (beach) 19, 40, 41

Kamini Beach 41
Kangatika 39, 42
Kloni Gouli Beach 41
Kipiadi (beach) **40-1**, 43
Kipos (beach) 10, 17, 40, 42, 43
Koutsi **14**, 17, 35
Lakka 7, 10, **18**, 22, 23, 44, 47, 48, 51, 53, 54, 55, **cover**
  bus timetable 7
  Cape Lakka 10, 18, 54, 55
Lakkos (bay and beach) 52
Levrechio (beach) 17, 40, **42-3**
Loggos **4-5**, 7, 10, 12, **17**, 35, 39, 40, 43, 48, **52**
  bus timetable 7
Magazia 11, 12, 16, 19, 20, 44, 46
Makratika 9, 15, **32**, **34**
Marmari (beach) 35, 40, 43
Messovrika (beach, Antipaxos) 10, 59, 63
Missorachi (beach) 10, **56-7**
Moggonissi (island) 8, **9**, 13, 14, 15, 22, 26, 28, **30-1**
Monodendri (beach) **49**, **50**, 51
Mouzmouli (bay and cliffs) 8, **14**, 26, 28
Orkos (bay and beach) 48, 53
Ozias 8, 12, 15, 30
Plani (beach) 54, **55**, 56
Tripitos (arch) 26, **27**, 29
Vassiliatika 54, 57
Vellianitatika 8, 15, 26, 28, **32**, 33
Vigla (Antipaxos) 59, 60
Vlachopoulatika 16, 44
Voutoumi (beach, Antipaxos) 10, 59, **61**, **62-3**
Vrika (Antipaxos) 10, 59, 60
Zernatika 39, 42